WISE WOMEN SPEAK

20 WAYS
TO TURN
STUMBLING
BLOCKS
INTO
STEPPING
STONES

WISE WOMEN SPEAK

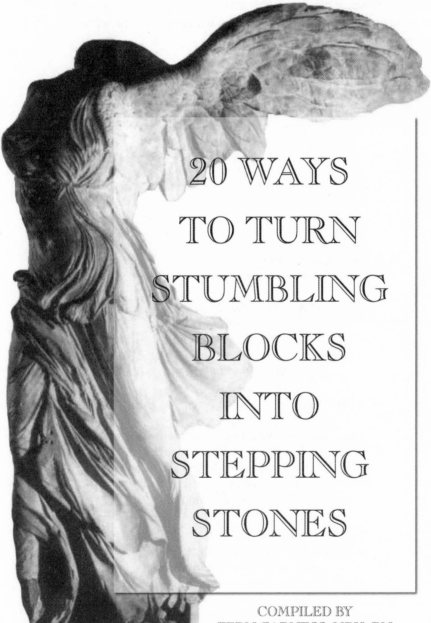

20 WAYS TO TURN STUMBLING BLOCKS INTO STEPPING STONES

COMPILED BY
FERN CARNESS, MPH, RN

CARNESS HEALTH MANAGEMENT, LLC
LAKE OSWEGO, OREGON

Cover: The Winged Victory of Samothrace, a Greek masterpiece in marble, represents the goddess of victory alighting upon the prow of a war galley, triumphant in conflict, her wings still beating in airy grace yet flowing with serenity and strength, is housed in The Louvre, Paris.

Permission granted from John M. Walcott, Walcott Studio to print the photograph of Ada-Reva Franklin on page 51.

Cover design by Lou Anne Zacek, L A Design Co.,
www.ladesignco.com
Editor: Sandra Wendel (www.health-eheadlines.com)
Text design by Sheryl Mehary
Winged Victory image, concept and historical research
by Jackie Mauritz of Electric Loft
Printing by Electric Loft

Carness Health Management, LLC

P.O. Box 509
Lake Oswego, Oregon 97034
503-636-7513

Contents

Introduction

I believe that there are no coincidences in the universe. Everything happens for a reason. The authors here have come together for a reason, whether we know what it is or not. Maybe we are here merely for your complete enjoyment. Or to help you overcome your stumbling blocks and turn them into stepping-stones.

Wise Women Speak is a compilation of stories from 20 different strong and amazing women. Although none of these women considers herself "wise," I find that each one has a compelling story that comes from her personal experience and allows the sharing of wisdom learned along the way. In each section the author has been exquisitely honest to allow you, the reader, to see inside her heart. Here lie the challenges and triumphs that create a unique sense of knowing in each woman. It is in the sharing of that wisdom that we all grow just a little wiser. And you, dear reader, become wise too, like Winged Victory, the goddess of our cover.

Perhaps you purchased this book because you heard one of the authors speak. Or you were given this book as a loving gift. No matter how it came to be in your hands at this moment in time, I invite you to find a story that particularly touches you, because you most certainly will.

Here's how these stories came together: Many of these coauthors share their experiences from the podium and make their livelihood, in part, by speaking professionally to public groups. Each woman was asked to contribute a chapter that is also consistent with a topic that they speak about. This way, when the author is on the platform and speaking, those in the audience, who choose, can take away with them a piece of the experience to re-read or to share with others. I adapted this book project from a similar concept Doug Smart used with other speakers.

The notion is that with 20 people financing the project it becomes an affordable publishing venture. Thus each person can have a book to display her work, while at the same time supporting the work of other women. This is a very rare collaborative and communal business model. I'm a speaker myself and wanted a book to showcase myself and my topics. But when I hatched this project, I was not even sure I could find 20 women to participate.

At first I sent out requests to women that I personally know whom, like myself, speak in the area of health and wellness. One by one the authors self-selected to participate. But our network is strong and more far-reaching than I ever imagined. Emails and telephone calls came from women I did not know asking about the book and how they might participate. Thus this book was born.

Sit back, sip a cup of tea, relax and enjoy!

With your health in mind,

Fern Carness

Medicine From the Inside Out
7 Keys to Unlock Your Natural Healing Wisdom

Karen Wolfe, MBBS, MA

Karen Wolfe is a licensed physician from her homeland, Australia, and is a certified Medical Hypnotherapist and Life Coach. She holds a master's degree in psychology and is passionate about the mind-body connection in health and disease. She is in great demand as a professional speaker, author, and coach. She has written seven books including *Give Stress A Rest, From Stress to Strength,* and *Successful Aging and Menopause.*

A complete description of the seven keys presented here is available as a four-tape audiobook, *Medicine From the Inside Out* available from her Web site.

Dr. Karen Wolfe
(949) 581-3269 phone and fax
www.drkarenwolfe.com
info@drkarenwolfe.com

Karen Wolfe

My Story

My childhood dream was to be on the Australian Olympic swimming team. My loving and supportive family instilled in me the belief that I could achieve anything if I was willing to work hard and believe that I could do it. I reached the state training squad for the 1976 Montreal Olympic swimming team in my final year of high school.

Fearing that the Olympics would distract me from the hard study I needed to prepare for life, I gave up my place on the team so I could study to gain entry into medical school. In Australia only the top 2% of students get an opportunity to go.

I remember a feeling of divine discontent throughout my medical training. I took a year off halfway through to be a travel guide in Sydney, and loved it! I felt free and open to new experiences, I did finish medical school, yet the next two years of internship and residency were hard. The long hours, isolation, sleep deprivation, hospital hierarchy, and exposure to terminal illness all took their toll.

I went into general practice after my residency and then became a medical adviser to the Australian Health Department on aged care issues. This work gave me the opportunity to speak, travel, and create change in an organization. After an executive training program, I became Medical Director of the Australian Government Health Service.

My life path then took another dramatic turn. In December 1990, I was at a conference in Anaheim, Calif., and met an American man! Our long-distance relationship allowed us to really get to know each other at a soul level. We fell very much in love and knew we wanted to be together, so I left the life I knew to explore the unknown. The road less traveled was certainly the name of this adventure. I left my profession, my country, my family, and all that was familiar... for love!

It took courage and a willingness to step into the unknown. I have never looked back. Following my heart at that time was the bravest and boldest thing I have ever done. It was a great lesson for me in stepping out and following my intuition.

Steve and I married in 1992. My first job in the United States was doing body fat screenings for an HMO. This was a major change from my medical career. I became a stepmother to two beautiful American children aged 9 and 4. I look back at that time and realize that love was the guiding light for me. With an open heart I was able to overcome any obstacle. My family became the foundation and purpose of my life.

I completed my master's degree in psychology and was fascinated by the mind-body connection in health and disease. Our daughter, Kelsey Grace, was born in 1993 and another part of me flowered. Being a mother has been the greatest gift of all and has opened my heart even further. For the next seven years I worked in preventive health care where I challenged individuals to become active partners in their health care needs.

All of these experiences then led me to a deep interest and passion for integrative medicine — a form of healing that recognized the mind, spirit, emotions, and body as interrelated in health and disease. I began to realize what was missing from my medical school training and became passionate about communicating this message to health professionals and audiences around the world.

I began my own company called Healing Quest. I felt the fear of having my own business, but again my heart knew what I needed to do. I have the delight of consulting with companies on integrative medicine, writing, speaking, coaching, and practicing hypnotherapy. I travel throughout the U.S. and Australia, speaking about a new vision for healing that embraces mind, body, and spirit. My medical training gives me the background to bring strong scientific evidence to this relatively new area of medicine.

Every day is a balancing act. My family is my foundation, my spiritual principles support my life path, and I go out in the world with a clear understanding of what I am meant to do. Each day is a gift. I am so blessed to be living my purpose as a mother, wife, speaker, coach, and author. The following saying is one that was sent to me by my very special Canadian friend. I have held these words close to my heart on my journey to turn stumbling blocks into stepping-stones.

It costs so much to be a full human being and there are very few who have the enlightenment or the courage to pay the price. One has to abandon the search for security, and with both arms reach out to the risk of living.

One has to embrace the world like a lover.

- One has to accept that pain is a condition of existence.
- One has to court doubt and darkness as the costs of knowing.
- One needs a will stubborn in conflict, but always in the total acceptance of every consequence of living and dying.

Medicine From the Inside Out
7 Keys to Unlock Your Natural Healing Wisdom

Our bodies are wired to benefit from exercising not only our muscles but our rich inner, human core — our beliefs, values, thoughts and feelings.

Herbert Benson, MD

How do our beliefs affect our health? Are our bodies and minds distinct from each other or do they function together as parts of an interconnected system? Because beliefs and emotions are largely ephemeral and imperceptible, Western medicine has largely assumed that their effects are neither physical nor measurable. Western medical science, in its passion to preserve life, has neglected the motivations that drive us, the meaning of life that makes people thirst for health and longevity.

The journey of *Medicine from the Inside Out* is an awakening of your deeper self — your invisible and indestructible reality — your essence identity. *Medicine From the Inside Out* will help you to identify the patterns of your life and the deep interconnection of your mind, body, and spirit. The seven keys to unlock your natural healing wisdom are the critical regulators of the flow of your life energy.

The Molecules of Emotion and Belief

Emotions and beliefs exist in the body as informational chemicals. As neurobiologist Candace Pert has proven, neuropeptides, the chemicals triggered by emotions, are thoughts converted into matter. Thoughts are things, and mental phenomena are messengers bringing information and intelligence from the non-physical world to the body. We store emotions and beliefs in our physical body, and they interact with our cells and tissues. The body becomes the battlefield for the war games of the mind. Unresolved emotions are held, embodied, and show up in the body as illness. Dr. Pert tells us we can no longer separate the mind from the body and that the mind is in every cell of the body. Our emotional energy converts into biological matter through a highly complex process.

Your Personality and Your Health

Scientists have long known that people with certain tempera-
ments are more prone to certain diseases. For example, excessive
hostility is associated with heart disease. Each of the seven keys
corresponds to a certain universal set of emotions and specific
memories of individual life experiences. Each key also corresponds
to a stage of psychological and emotional development where
memories are laid down and resonate at specific frequencies within
your body.

As you grow through life, these keys are formed in a continuous
building process. The nature of the key and its significance to your
health is determined in much the same way your personality is determined by the experiences you have in your life. As you explore the
keys, you can begin to see how your personality and life experiences are intertwined with your health.

Energy Anatomy

Quantum physicists have confirmed the reality of the basic
vibratory essence of life. The physical body that you can see and feel
and touch is only an outer shell. To tap into your unlimited
potential, you need to feel your body from within, to feel the life
inside your body and thereby come to know that you are beyond
the outer form.

The idea of a fundamental energy force flowing through us
has been a mainstay of Eastern thought for millennia. The Indians
describe this absolute energy as *prana*, the Chinese and Japanese
refer to the universal life energy force *chi*, which is the source of all
energy and whose flows are responsible for who we are.

Just as Western medicine has a detailed physical anatomical
system, so too does Energy Medicine. You might think of it as an
echo of your physical body, always moving, occupying the same
"space," only on a different, subtler level. As you step into this world
of energy, you will develop a new understanding of "energy
anatomy." The energy body has its own complex shape and form.
Unlike the physical body that you see with the naked eye, the
energy body is in constant flux, ever flowing and changing. For this
reason, different observers see it in different ways. As a result, there
are a variety of possible "maps" of the energy body.

The Human Biocomputer

Although the idea of an absolute energy force is central to many spiritual traditions, it is perhaps the ancient system of the seven energy centers — vortices of energy — that offers the most accessible and immediately practical approach to understanding this force and the way it works. According to ancient Indian teachings, these seven energy centers, or *chakras* (which means *disk*), govern the generation and processing of energy in order to maintain our physical, emotional, and spiritual systems. The *chakras* were first described by Eastern, Egyptian, and Native American spiritual traditions that date back at least 20,000 years.

The *chakras* are each located at a spot along the body's spinal column and are associated with specific emotional and physical processes. Although they cannot be seen or held as material entities, they are evident in the shape of our physical bodies, the patterns manifested in our lives, and how we think, feel, and handle life situations. They take in energy and information and consciousness that is all around us and process and distribute it to our physical, emotional, mental, and spiritual energy bodies. Each *chakra* processes energy that corresponds to specific physical, emotional, mental, and spiritual aspects of our being.

How appropriate that in modern times disks are a common storage unit of programmed information. The analogy of the Internet and our computer age is a visual way to look at these seven energy centers and the energetic body. Each of the components of a computer can be used to explain the map of your energy anatomy.

- **Hardware** = the physical body. The densest aspect of one's spiritual, emotional, and physical energy.

- **Software** = our energetic programming. We did not write all of these programs, and some of the language is no longer useful. A major challenge is to identify the programs that are no longer useful and rewrite them while living a rich, full life. This is the task of healing.

- **User** = the Self

- **Information Storage** (disks) = the seven keys to unlock your natural healing wisdom that contain specific information about our physical, emotional, mental, and spiritual energy. The information is embodied in developmental stages throughout life and laid down as energetic vibrations in specific parts of your body and aggregated as follows:

Key 1   Your Fundamental Grounding of Beliefs and Values

Key 2   Relationships and Control Issues

Key 3   Personal Power

Key 4   Love

Key 5   Communication

Key 6   Intuition

Key 7   Spirituality

- **Electricity** = the flow of energy through our system.

- **Virus** = distractions from our true path often play a part in not letting us access the deeper parts of ourselves.

- **World Wide Web** = our deep inner knowing or intuition that is an invisible information network. It has limitless potential that can be used to access information if we know how to get connected and where to find the information.

The 7 Keys for Renewal

These seven keys will unlock your natural healing wisdom and create a renewal for your mind, body, and spirit. I have taken the word *renewal* and used each letter of the word to represent one of the keys. Let us explore each key so you can begin your renewal into health and healing.

KEY NUMBER 1 — Release Limiting Beliefs

Many of us define ourselves by our past. Every memory and belief is stored or "embodied" in the cells of your body. The first key has to do with the base of support we experience in the family. From conception to age 1, we learn to trust and feel safe and to help ourselves or feel helpless. Healing in this key is about examining your fundamental beliefs and changing the ones that do not help you grow in order to improve the health of your immune system, skeleton, lower back, blood, and support structures.

Developmental Stage	Conception to age 1
Location	Base of the spine
Body Organs	Physical body support, lower back, bones, immune system
Physical Dysfunction	Chronic lower back pain, depression, immune system disorders
Emotional Issues	Sense of belonging to a group, physical safety, and security
Primary Fear	Fears of physical survival and abandonment by the group
Color	Red

Healing Questions

- What belief patterns did you inherit from your family?
- Which of these belief patterns still have authority in your thinking?
- What family traditions do you continue for yourself or your family?

KEY NUMBER 2 — Examine Your Relationships and Your Ego

This key is double sided. The first side is related to what drives us in life and to holding on versus letting go. The other side regulates our relationships with others and our sexuality. We learn to create methods to control our lives such as challenging authority and other people.

Developmental Stage	Ages 2–4 years (the potty training years!)
Location	Navel area
Body Organs	Sexual organs, large intestine, pelvis, bladder and appendix
Physical Dysfunction	Female reproductive disorders, sexual potency, urinary problems
Emotional Issues	Power and control, creativity, money, and sex

Primary Fear	Fear of losing control or being controlled by others
Color	Orange

Healing Questions

* Do you consider yourself a creative person? Do you follow through on your creative ideas?
* Are you comfortable with your sexuality?
* Are you a controlling person? Do you engage in power plays in your relationships?
* Does money have authority over you?
* What goals do you have for yourself that you have yet to pursue? What stands in the way of your acting upon those goals?

KEY NUMBER 3 — Nurture Self-Esteem

This is the center of your personal power. Self-esteem is essential for good health. This key determines the quality of our lives and our capacity to succeed in business, relationships, and healing. People with low self-esteem attract relationships and situations that reflect and reinforce this low self-esteem and vise versa.

Developmental Stage	Ages 3–5 years
Location	Solar plexus
Body Organs	Stomach, pancreas, gallbladder, liver, kidneys, adrenals, upper intestines
Physical Dysfunction	Gastric ulcers, colon/intestinal problems, diabetes, indigestion, hepatitis, anorexia
Emotional Issues	Trust, self-confidence, self-respect, responsibility, fear, and intimidation
Color	Yellow

Healing Questions

* Do you like yourself? If not, what don't you like about yourself?

- Are you critical of others?

- Do you need the approval of others?

- Are you able to admit it when you are wrong?

- Have you ever allowed yourself to be in a relationship with a person you didn't really love, but it seemed better than being alone?

- Are you afraid of responsibility? Or do you feel responsible for everyone and everything?

KEY NUMBER 4– Express Emotions

Located at the heart, this key processes emotions such as love, judgment, trust, courage, hostility, resentment and forgiveness. Judging, controlling, and manipulating constrict this area, while surrender, courage, appreciation, and gratitude expand it. This fourth key is the doorway to transformation.

Developmental Stage	Ages 4–7 years
Location	Heart
Body Organs	Heart and circulatory system, lungs, breasts, diaphragm, ribs, shoulders
Physical Dysfunction	Heart disease, asthma/allergy, breast disease/cancer, lung cancer,
Emotional Issues	Love and hatred, resentment, grief and anger, forgiveness, compassion, hope
Color	Green

Healing Questions

- What emotional memories do you still need to heal?

- How do you express anger and hostility?

- What is your understanding of forgiveness? Who are the people you have yet to forgive, and what prevents you from letting go of the pain you associate with them?

- What is your understanding of a healthy, intimate relationship?

KEY NUMBER 5 — Words and Willpower Matter

This key regulates our ability to speak the truth. Keeping your word is very valued in our culture. This key feeds energy into the thyroid gland, which in turn affects metabolism and issues of timing.

Developmental Stage	Ages 7–12 years
Location	Throat
Body Organs	Throat, thyroid, mouth, neck vertebrae, teeth, gums, parathyroid, trachea
Physical Dysfunction	Chronic sore throat, mouth ulcers, gum disease, laryngitis, scoliosis, thyroid problems, TMJ, swollen glands
Emotional Issues	Personal expression, addiction, will-power, following one's dream, criticism
Color	Blue

Healing Questions

- Are you able to express yourself honestly and openly when you need to? If not, why not?
- What makes you lose control of your own willpower?
- Who are the people in your life that have control over your willpower, and why?

KEY NUMBER 6 — Attitude Matters

Also known as the "third eye," this key is the center of our mental and intuitive abilities. Within the Eastern spiritual literature, this is the spiritual center in which the interaction of mind and psyche can lead to wisdom. The key is to create an attitude or "posture" of openness to change and the ability to see the purpose for your life.

Developmental Stage	Adolescence
Location	Center of forehead, slightly above the eyes

Body Organs	Brain, nervous system, eyes, ears, nose, pituitary gland, pineal gland
Physical Dysfunction	Blindness, deafness, seizures, spinal disorders, learning disabilities
Emotional Issues	Openness to ideas of others, emotional intelligence, truth
Color	Indigo

Healing Questions

- What attitudes do you have that disempower you?

- What beliefs and attitudes would you like to change in yourself?

- Are you open to receiving guidance and insight through your dreams?

- Do you believe that success in life means achieving certain goals? Can you visualize success in life as an energy force not a physical one?

- Do you act on your inner guidance? Do you need "proof" that your inner guidance is authentic?

KEY NUMBER 7 — Let Go and Let Grace

This key is our connection to our spiritual nature and to the transcendent dimension of life.

Developmental Stage	Throughout life
Location	Crown of the head
Body Organs	Major body systems, muscular system, skin
Physical Dysfunction	Chronic fatigue syndrome, energetic disorders, depression
Emotional Issues	Transcendent ideas, humanitarianism, faith, spirituality, and devotion
Color	Violet

Healing Questions

- Are you devoted to a particular spiritual path? If not, do you feel a need to find one?

- What questions have you sought guidance with during meditation or moments of prayer?

- What questions have you asked that seek insight into your life's purpose?

- What fears do you have related to your understanding of God?

The Keys in Action

The keys are not separate from each other. In fact, the less interactive they are, the less integrated you will be physically, emotionally, mentally, and spiritually. Your entire body is a resonating device and the keys are in intimate relationship with your physical body. Information that comes into each key also gets stored in the body. For example, the liver often holds our unresolved anger; the kidneys, our fear; the pancreas, our ability to digest sweetness in life, and so on.

The value of understanding your energy anatomy is to be able to seek the energy meaning of a situation, and understand when, where, and why you are losing energy. Always keep in mind the seven keys of renewal to unlock your natural healing wisdom.

1. **Release Limiting Beliefs**
2. **Examine Your Relationships**
3. **Nurture Self-esteem**
4. **Express Your Emotions**
5. **Words and Willpower Matter**
6. **Attitude Matters**
7. **Let Go and Let Grace**

Simple and powerful, these keys will help you focus your mind, body, and spirit. Through this self-evaluation you will develop the skill of reading your energy body and sensing your intuitive guidance.

Carry the Torch High
Keys to Coaching Great Performance

Jan Carothers, CPC

Through keynote speeches, seminars, and leadership coaching, Jan Carothers incites and encourages participants to stretch and achieve extraordinary performance. That's her goal: to inspire people to action. Many think of her as The Torch Lady — for the torch of purpose, leadership, service, and fun she holds high and passes on to her audiences.

As co-author of *Hiring Champions* and as a Certified Personnel Consultant, Jan draws on her success in recruiting, managing, and training to provide timely, useful information to help leaders across most industries overcome external barriers and self-imposed limitations to meet their highest goals.

In her own business for over 13 years, she serves business and nonprofit client audiences through topics including Coaching Great Performance, Delighting Your Customers, Being Memorable, Attracting and Keeping a Winning Team: Hiring Champions, and Stretching Yourself to Teamwork.

She is a native Oregonian with a BA in theater. Out of her fascination with the Great Western Migration, she gives a keynote performance called Reclaim Your Pioneer Spirit: Leadership Guides from the Oregon Trail. As a Wagon Train Woman, she tells about making the long journey to achieve life-changing goals.

Jan especially cares about the challenges of nonprofit, mission-driven organizations in the arts and social services and annually conducts several board and staff team-building, leadership, and planning retreats. Among her coaching clients are board presidents and executive directors. A Professional Member of the National Speakers Association, Jan is also a board member of the National Speakers Association-Oregon.

In 1988 while co-founding a community mentoring program for high-risk youth called Committed Partners for Youth, Jan fell in love and married her co-founder Jeff Bornefeld. Together they served CPY as volunteers in fundraising and program leadership for over 13 years concurrent with their consulting, training, and speaking careers.

The Torch Lady
Jan Carothers, CPC
PO Box 2094
Portland, OR 97208-2094
(503) 786-9132
(503) 786-1794 fax
thetorchlady@jancarothers.com
www.jancarothers.com

My Story

Carry Your Own Torch

One of our jobs in life is to do our best to be a light, to "Carry the Torch" for others. We lend support to each other to make good choices that take us closer to the lives we all want -- filled with love, accomplishment, and peace.

I have always wanted to be a leader, to help others to see what's possible for them, to assist them to discover how much is available in life. Through my lifetime quest for love, grace, beauty, and stability, I began to realize that before I could authentically serve and influence others, first I had to wake up and grasp my own life. I couldn't just blithely talk; I had to walk the very challenging walk.

My path to courageous living felt daunting because I had to awaken to all my own self-imposed, protective limitations — chosen consciously or unconsciously. I had to overcome the denial that everything in my past was just fine and start taking big uncomfortable risks. If I would ever be an example for others, I would have to stop being just a giver of good advice and become instead a passionate torch to overcome my own resistance, defensiveness, and fear.

After college, I discovered I had serious emotional work to do. With the help of a therapist, and other introspective activities, I saw how confusing my childhood had been. My mother tried to fulfill her needs, and mine, as she saw them, looking for love in a stable marriage. Sadly, it was a goal she achieved only briefly, several times with several mates. Along the way, I adapted to my mother's life and was shaped by her choices and needs, long before I discovered my own. I was an only child until age 10 when Mom married again creating a patchwork family composed of a fascinating stepfather and 5 of us children, who were each influenced by our various parents' total of 11 marriages.

Understandably, I decided that marriage itself was a disaster — that I could be abandoned by people I loved and betrayed by people I trusted. Though I grew to love my put-together family, it was not without serious troubles. We had one hyperactive-borderline-alcoholic little brother, one mildly retarded little sister, one older brother who stole and crashed the family car and later, at 17, ran away to the Navy, one "summer" brother who lived with his mother, and me, the passive-aggressive sister trying to be "good." All of us were mavericks, holding on tight in this carnival ride of a family. For me there was an additional grave influence. I worked summers from age 13 to 19 for my stepdad in his office. During that continuous exposure, he overstepped the limits of parental affection into seduction, leading me into the wildly confusing, nonviolent yet damaging, wrong yet "romantic," alienating and hurtful life of secret, incestuous sex.

One Christmas, when clearing our forest road my charismatic stepfather was killed in an icy, tractor accident — devastating me and freeing me from my upsetting required secrecy. The high drama of his death finally unraveled the cords that kept this loosely connected clan together. After I traumatically confessed what had gone on, my mother and I went through six years of polite distance. After those chilly superficial years, we began to reclaim and rebuild a forgiving, trusting relationship, owning our own accountabilities for what happened, and ultimately forgiving my stepfather's betrayals.

Yet, my life was never one-dimensional! Along with all the craziness, there were genuine affection and generous resources. I had the advantage of receiving a great education, and I learned to work. Better than that, I learned about service from my folk's activities in our mountain community. I learned about leadership and about guiding groups to do great work together. My mom and dad, in effect, were stars in our community.

My childhood provided the "background music" of my life. My interests provided the focus: how to be committed, serve others, be artistic, be loving, carry my weight, earn my place in the group or community, and make the world better.

Unfortunately, I developed the basic viewpoint that "no matter what I do, it's never enough." Most of us have some version of this theme running in our lives. We scramble to do better, yet we rarely acknowledge, appreciate, and in some cases forgive what we've done.

Now, I finally understand that unless I allow myself the fruit of my work, the enjoyment and self-acknowledgment of good effort and its results, no one else can ever feel wholly peaceful around me.

The old proverb is true — "to love others, first love yourself." I came to realize I had a lot of grief work to do, and I needed to invest the time to do it. I had to stop submerging myself in leading volunteer organizations and causes so I could finally set my own life on course.

Slowly a miracle began to occur. The ultimate paradox! I discovered nothing was broken. There was nothing to fix! This was and is the key for me. Truly the only thing missing was accepting, loving, and taking care of myself.

Along the way several things occurred to have my life take a turn for the extraordinary. I accepted that I could, in fact, have a life filled with love, accomplishment, and service. For its own sake. Not to justify and rationalize my existence. I let in a wonderful man who is the perfect partner for *real* life. Amazing to me, I, the woman who would never, ever get married, would never really trust a man, have been married happily for over 12 years.

Another extraordinary win for me was to withdraw from compulsive volunteer leadership for a long sabbatical to rest and focus on inner work. As long as I crusaded on good causes, I could avoid leading and living my best life. Through that experience, I now see glimmers of inner peace that allow me to relax and focus on my own professional work instead of on everything that *must* be done to change the world. Now, when I take on projects, it is an addition to, not an escape from, my life. Life doesn't have to be *either/or*, it can include what I choose.

I've had to give up a black and white view of myself and the world. I'm not good or bad, right or wrong, enough or not. I can look at myself and others on a continuum in which every quality is present. This takes carrying my own torch and accepting light from the torches of others. It has taken waking up to some areas of illusion and denial, and reckoning with the basic pains of being human. We all have inner voices nagging us. We all have had to struggle to find our peaceful center. We all have our own gifts and life challenges. We all must let others in — despite our fear of risk.

I am not the best, nor the worst, only completely my uniquely sufficient self. There will always be self-improvements I'd like to make, but nothing is required for me to deserve my own love and respect. And from this simple place, I can hold my torch high.

Carry The Torch High
Keys to Coaching Great Performance

If everyone in your group performed as a champion, what could you accomplish together? How would you feel to have all of them come to their work and projects alive, energized, and extending themselves beyond self-imposed limits? What would you give to have your people doing their very best work and stretching up to their highest potential?

Most of us know we have room to grow, but few are eager to leave behind familiar, comfortable behaviors in favor of challenging new approaches. That, however, is the key to becoming an effective coach; finding ways to help others make changes and let go of the accustomed in favor of an unfamiliar yet better future.

Greek philosopher Plutarch said, "The mind is not a vessel to be filled, but a fire to be kindled!" What a useful guide in coaching great performance! It calls us to remember that each person carries an inner fire and an inner knowing waiting for support. Our job, as coach, is not to pour forth our great wisdom to those we coach. Rather it is to identify each individual's own goals, and then provide the support and inspiration to spark, fuel, and fan the flames of passion, inspiration, and creativity in each person we lead.

These are demanding times! As pressures increase to tighten expenses and rise above the stress, it's important in your role as a leader to stay aware of a higher purpose, and of the vision you hold for your organization and each person in it.

To optimize the talent of your colleagues who have demanding workloads in competitive markets, you can give them a stronger edge by becoming a better coach. Coaching is an evolving style of management support, adapted from sports, that can be used to great benefit by associates at all levels to manifest their primary values of client service, productivity, profitability, and professional development.

Carry the torch for others

Every Olympic year, we're reminded of the enormous power of that most famous torch as it is held high in the night sky. Such symbols of excellence can reach deep into our hearts and draw forth our individual visions of possibility. As the torchbearers circle the globe, running beyond where they'd like to stop, they call us into action. They ignite our own visions and transform them into a creative action plan. One crucial role of the coach is to "hold up the torch" for your people, to carry it to remind them, in the face of daily pressures, the shared core values of the work you do together.

As a manager, whatever the work, you're in a unique position to influence and lead people to a greater level of excellence and satisfaction while meeting the needs and requirements of your organization. You will personally benefit by becoming a more caring and persuasive coach. You will increase your productivity, profitability, and creativity in your work, family, and community as you enhance the results of those around you.

What made your great coaches great?

Think of a person in your life who extended himself or herself for you and positively influenced your development. Whether he or she was an early boss, a colleague, a teacher, a relative, a minister, a scout leader, or an actual team coach, he or she played a coaching role for you. What made that coach so memorable? Our best coaches had most of these qualities:

- Held high performance expectations
- Communicated clearly
- Appreciated us and wanted us to succeed
- Trusted and respected us
- Cared about what we wanted to accomplish
- Deserved our trust, respect, and loyalty
- Saw the best in us, even before we could see it
- Were inspiring models
- Asked great questions that prompted us to find our own solutions
- Listened well
- Gave us freedom to take risks and try out new skills
- Provided a safety net from high-risk consequences
- Gave useful feedback
- Maintained a nurturing focused environment

- Had a sense of humor and perspective
- Found us worth their time
- Made themselves accessible

What causes people to stretch and grow?

Smart coaches know that people work for their own benefit, whether tangible or intangible, as well as for the benefit of others. It's evident that people respond more favorably to suggestions, requests, ideas, even correction, when they are fully engaged in something they care about and believe it is in their own best interest.

Coaching people effectively is an art that draws on your personal skills of trust and relationship building, communication, and persuasion. Coaching is engaging another's compelling interests, sparking their internal motivations, expanding their willingness to stretch and grow, and enhancing their visions of the future. Effective coaching calls out our best, most courageous selves. It helps us to align with the mission of the organization we serve and encourages us to go beyond where we might want to stop.

Why do we want to become coaches?

These days the competition for great people is tough. No matter how many people are available, we really must keep seeking and keeping the best.

Most employees, like volunteers, are looking for meaning and intangible rewards from their work along with good compensation. Each of us wants to think that our time and efforts were useful and mattered to others. If you're in an endeavor in which your people know they will be treated fairly and respectfully; that they will develop, participate and flourish in their work; and that their work serves a useful human purpose, they will not be easily lured away.

Unfortunately many managers see coaching only as an activity to correct undesirable or inadequate employee behavior, so it is infrequently used with their good and excellent employees. Because your best employees already do their jobs well, they may receive little or no coaching to influence them to expand and grow.

Treat employees like volunteers

Many people say, "Our employees are our most important asset." Yet not everyone who says it lives it. If you've ever had to search hard to hire a good employee, you know it is true. If you're fortunate enough to have great people working for you, consider this idea. Treat your employees like volunteers in a well-run volunteer organization. They will recognize that you acknowledge the importance of their receiving value from their work beyond their compensation. That value comes from doing work that gives them pride, with colleagues who share important values, who appreciate and respect them.

With coaching, your people are able to express more of their creativity and enthusiasm, and to reach their own stated goals. As you become an effective coach, your people can become effective teams. There are not too many places in modern life where people actually get to experience genuine connection and effectiveness in groups. An empowering, spirited workplace is a rare and wonderful thing. With intention and skill you can create one.

Personal investment of the coach

What must the manager who wishes to become a great coach invest? It will "cost" having all the answers and sharing all our hard-won wisdom. While we can share some of it, people generally don't develop as fully from being given our methods, our answers, or our advice.

Borrowing the sports metaphor, being a coach implies that someone else must develop the skills to actually play the game. Coaching is a different and necessary skill, the skill to see and bring out the best in the talents of others. So, you don't have to have all the answers. In fact, you shouldn't.

What you do need to think about is the quality of the questions you ask. People either grow and flourish under caring thoughtful, well-designed, targeted, open-ended questioning or they feel intimidated and interrogated. Everything depends on your set-up of the coaching relationship and the trust level the person feels for you.

To be a coach is to be part practitioner of practical management wisdom, part committed cheerleader, part guidance counselor, part rigorous "tough guy," and part supportive friend.

If you can see the value of continuously developing a team of exceptional people, delivering extraordinary results and loving it, you may want to embark on a path of coaching mastery.

12 Keys to Coaching Great Performance

1. Strive to create an atmosphere of encouragement, clarity, camaraderie, and competence. Examine your beliefs. Transform any of your underlying opinions that employees must be controlled and policed. If you've assembled good people, your job as coach is to empower them; to identify their best qualities and amplify their strengths; and assist them to set and achieve their own professional and personal, as well as the group's, goals. Have them identify objectives and outcomes they are deeply committed to achieving.

2. Plan to invest sufficient time to build a relationship with every individual you coach, and to understand the person's inner motivations, commitments, and goals. Be authentically committed to their achieving their goals and be willing to let your people know it. The exceptional coach is honest and open.

3. Recognizing that most performance can be improved, the coach heartily acknowledges current accomplishments and still cultivates a spirit of constructive dissatisfaction in the group that inspires continuous improvement without making the "game" seem impossible to win.

4. Ask for the permission of each individual you are coaching. It is smart not to presume their permission. Granting permission to be coached "in the moment," the employee is reaffirming his or her own responsibility for achieving the results. You must deserve and gain their trust. It is the most important factor that will allow the individual to give permission to be coached and to take personal risks, to experiment, and grow. Keep your word, keep people informed and, when in doubt, tell the truth.

5. Implement a performance review process that supports a mutual appraisal of strengths and areas to enhance, develops performance goals for the year, and gives the manager a solid basis for coaching throughout the year. Set challenging goals — big enough to be inspiring and require a stretch. Make large requests. Be willing to look and stand for the potential in others.

6. Be willing to take risks with people. Experiment to find the best approach for each individual. Coaching is creative, people-centered management that combines communications technology with behavioral science and intuition, with few formulas and no guarantees.

7. Have tolerance for people making mistakes. Have "missed attempts" be forgivable and be opportunities for individual and team learning. Perceived lack of safety for error can suppress creativity, innovation, and risk taking.

8. Ask searching questions that open new areas of possibility, questions that assist people to discover powerful answers and new directions.

9. Hold your "players" accountable for the actions and results they promise. Also hold yourself accountable. Do not blame other people or circumstances for the results. Remember, you only succeed when your people succeed.

10. As the coach, you are responsible for the effectiveness and clarity of communication. Keep checking to see that your messages have been understood, and keep exploring new ways to communicate more clearly.

11. You must keep your focus on the vision as well as the detail. Powerful managers hold and communicate the mission and tailor coaching, energizing activities, rewards and recognition for each individual in the team. When performance slows, it's only the "larger picture," the shared values, that will re-ignite the fires of constructive action. Redirect and refocus people back to their own original purposes and reconnect their energy to fulfill the mission of the organization.

12. The only absolute formula for successfully coaching individuals is to keep trying things until something works. The final key is most important! Practice, Practice, Practice!

Most of us when considering our dreams, our highest potential, the things we'd really like to accomplish in this life, recognize that we are not going to get there alone. It will take others to share the vision and probably the work. There is very little that can be accomplished without the support of others. As a final suggestion I'd like to suggest as you Carry the Torch for others that you have fun and get *yourself* a great coach!

PARTNER to Empower ™

Fern Carness, MPH, RN, FAWHP

Fern Carness, MPH, RN, FAWHP, is a registered nurse with a background in critical care. Known as a voice for women's health, Fern travels extensively to speak to women's groups about health status and how to become empowered to partner with the health care system.

An entrepreneur at heart, Fern has founded four successful health care-related businesses. Invasive Diagnostic Specialists — a cardiac catheterization lab staff relief service provides high-caliber nurses to work in the area of invasive cardiology. This company was one of the first to recognize that nurses could work as independent contractors, bill fee-for-service, and function as businesswomen. Frustrated with the lack of health promotion in the hospital setting, Fern founded Wellness At Work, Inc., in 1986, a worksite health promotion company dedicated to improving the health status of individuals, one person at a time. For over 10 years, WAW provided Fern with the opportunity to reach thousands with her health promotion messages. After selling WAW to *Times Mirror* in 1995, Fern became Principal at Carness Health Management, LLC. CHM creates many health behavior change programs in print, video, audio, and Web format. Including **Ready Set STOP!** — a smoking cessation self-help program in both Web and audio formats and *A Wise Woman's Approach to Healing and Cancer.*

Currently, Fern is the co-owner of Just Like a Woman — a retail experience that blends specialty lingerie needs with health education and survivor support services in a feminine environment. Here women with medical challenges will find the products they need while being treated with dignity and kindness.

Whether sewing Halloween costumes, making heirloom quilts, trekking in the Himalayas, or dragon boating on the Willamette, Fern never sits still. While crewing a dragon boat, Fern and her breast cancer survivor teammates, known as Pink Phoenix, were awarded the Medal of Valor 2000 from the City of Portland when they rescued a man who had jumped off a bridge. Fern is a gold medal paddler who represented the United States Senior Women at the 4th World Dragon Boat Championships held in Philadelphia, August 2001.

Fern lives in Portland, Oregon, with her husband of over 32 years. Al and Fern have two sons and two beautiful granddaughters.

Fern Carness
Carness Health Management
(503) 636-7513
ferncarn@teleport.com

My Story

Doctor, you are the second opinion, my opinion counts!

I am a breast cancer survivor and my story is all too common. I was a trim, fit, and active 41-year-old. I had it all: a loving husband, two healthy growing sons, a successful business, and I had my health. Or so I thought. Then one morning in the shower I discovered a lump in my breast the size of a golf ball. I immediately knew that it was cancer! I stepped out of the shower and went right back into my life, never giving the lump a second thought. Later that evening my husband rediscovered the lump. Lights on, romance over!

I had just had a clean mammogram two months before, and no one in my family had had breast cancer, so I wasn't up for this. Yet deep inside there was a haunting whisper, "Fern, this is serious." So

I went to the doctor the next morning without even calling for an appointment. They squeezed me in and my ob-gyn examined me. Now this was not your average doctor-patient relationship. This doctor had delivered both of my children. He took care of all my friends and most of the nurses in town. He was a guardian angel to my sister. This doctor cared about me. Maybe too much, he did not want to see the obvious. Instead, he told me to keep an eye on the lump and come back after a couple of menstrual cycles. Relieved to hear the seemingly good news, I went home.

But by morning the whisper was shouting! This time I listened to my own intuition and went back again. This time I was sobbing so hard I could hardly speak as I demanded a needle biopsy. Dr. H. told me I was hysterical. He wanted to medicate me and call my husband to take me home. I told him, "Be that as it may, someone is going to put a needle in this right now, or I'll do it myself." So even though it was the Friday of a holiday weekend, a surgeon was called. I went upstairs to get a biopsy. Now, I'm a nurse, so when he popped the needle in there to aspirate, and he hit solid granite, I knew I was in trouble. He's saying, we'll send this off to pathology, and we'll call you Monday with the results, and thus followed the longest and the shortest weekend of my life.

I was supposed to work in the cardiac cath lab that Monday morning, but I had decided not to go in. However, one of the nurses called at 5 A.M. and said they had three cardiac emergencies and asked me to come in. I said I couldn't, I was waiting for some biopsy results. Like a typical nurse, she said, "Can't you wait for the results while you're working?" So, silencing the screaming whisper, I went to work. After a while my pager went off. It was the phone number of the surgeon. Why don't you come down, and we can go over your biopsy results and, by the way, could you bring a family member and all of your previous mammograms?

Now, I knew what this meant. I couldn't believe the ploy. Do they treat regular people this stupidly? I was terrified, but as a health educator, I was angry.

So my husband and I went to the surgeon's office. I was still in scrubs. I even had the blue booties over my sneakers. The surgeon told us the tumor was malignant and recommended a modified radical mastectomy. Then, as if I were no longer in the room, Dr. B. looked at my husband and said, "We'll have a plastic surgeon on standby. She'll go to sleep with two breasts, and she'll wake up with two breasts. You'll never even know she had cancer."

I said to the doctor, "Excuse me, but did anybody ask if I want to be reconstructed? You just told me I have cancer. I don't know exactly what that means to my life. I don't know whether I'm going to live or die, and you want to know if I want to have nice tits?"

He replied, "Fern, look how cute and sexy you are, and you're so young. Don't you want to still be like a woman?"

I guess the saddest part of this physician-patient encounter is that this doctor was very kind and meant this all with the greatest concern and best intentions. The man was genuinely trying to be helpful. He then said, "Well, if you like, you can get a second opinion…" And that's when I got angry.

I said, "Doctor, you **are** the second opinion. My opinion was first. I count here."

I wanted to find out whether reconstruction would make it harder to monitor for reoccurrence. I called five oncologists. With the first four, I couldn't get past the nurse because I wasn't *"referred by another doctor."* The fifth nurse said, "Dr. Charles would tell you, but he's on vacation and won't be back until Monday." This was Wednesday; I was having surgery on Thursday. But she called back an hour later and gave me the number of the doctor's brother, another physician.

I called and asked him my question. He nicely told me he understood my dilemma. "But I really can't advise you," he said. "I've never examined you. I haven't met you. I haven't seen your clinical situation. I just don't know what to say."

I said, "Okay, I understand. I'm a cardiovascular nurse specialist, and you sound to me like a short, balding, overweight, middle-aged guy and let me offer that if you get chest pain, and you're not sure whether you need an angioplasty, stents, TPA, CABG, or if you think you should just jump in and have a heart transplant, you give me a call. I'll at least give you my ballpark opinion."

After a brief pause, he said, "Don't get reconstructed." After which I said, "Thank you," and hung up.

Then, like all Jewish Princesses do when they have a major decision to make, I went to the mall!

The rest of the story is pretty basic. I had a modified radical mastectomy followed by six grueling months of chemotherapy during which I became committed to helping other women become their own first opinion. I wanted to teach them how to stand up for their own health care and to learn to trust their intuition, listen for the whisper.

The current status of my breast cancer is that I am doing well nine years later. Although I have had multiple biopsies on my remaining breast and ultimately a prophylactic mastectomy, everything has been benign. I have continued to take charge of my health by eating healthy and exercising regularly and mindfully. I have taken to daily practices that incorporate the mind, body, and spirit. I work in partnership with my doctors and providers to actively manage my health status. Remember, nobody knows your body like you do, listen to the whisper. Nobody cares about your health as much as you do. Get informed and be your own first opinion.

PARTNER to Empower™

Introduction to empowerment

Your health is your most valuable asset. No matter how many material things you have — cars, homes, clothes, jewelry, or other possessions — nothing really matters if you don't feel well. Nothing can replace the bounce in your step or the twinkle in your eye when you feel tiptop. Your physical, spiritual, emotional, and mental health depends on many things: your family genes, your medical care, your self-care habits, and your lifestyle.

Here is a framework for partnering with the health care system, if and when you need to, in order to manage a medical condition for you or your loved ones. But first, we will take a brief sidetrack and build a foundation of health and vitality that you can gain from healthy self-care routines and learning to listen to your body. Then I will explain the basic way the American health care system works and how to choose a doctor. Finally we will look at the health care decision-making model: PARTNER to Empower™.

As we embark on this new millennium, we see an upsurge of consumerism. Health care consumerism in particular. As the baby boomers age and chronic diseases become modern epidemics, our desire for medical information is huge. We want the information instantly, and we want it in a format that we can understand. Never before has health care been such a hot topic. And it is more than just your **right** to know, it is your **responsibility** to participate in your own health care decision-making and form a partnership with your health care team.

The mind-body connection

No one will ever know your body as well as you do. Every breath you take, every move you make is part of your body's history. In addition, current research proves that your body and your mind are not separate. What you think, what you feel, and what you do are all intricately combined to make you, you. Your biology is your biography.

Your body is a powerful healer. Many of your internal functions can help you prevent disease, manage illness, and even cure certain maladies. In fact it has been long known that when you take medicine, there are actually two reactions: one is the response of the pill itself determined by its chemical properties. The second and even more important is the belief you have in the pill's power and the confidence you have that it will help you. This is known as the placebo effect. So it is always helpful to expect the best outcome when you are getting medical treatments. The opposite of the placebo effect is the nocebo effect, which is the bad outcome that happens when you expect the worse. This is also an important factor to consider when choosing a doctor. A doctor who has a healthy, positive "can-do" attitude is more likely to help you heal than a doctor who believes that your condition is hopeless.

I recommend that you take a few minutes each day to do a quick body scan to see how you are feeling. This head-to-toe assessment is not a search–and-destroy mission, but rather a way for you to check in to see how well things are going. Learning to awaken your intuition is a very helpful step in mind-body healing. Your body speaks to you in a language that you need to learn. Taking a few minutes to listen to your body each day will help you hear more clearly your inner voice. If you don't listen to the whisper, your body will eventually shout in the form of pain, disability, or disease.

Self-care

Taking care of you is job number one. And yet in our busy work-a-day world it is easy to let our self-care habits fall by the wayside.

People get sick because of a unique combination of factors: genetics, family characteristics, environment, life experiences, weather and exposures to germs, viruses, or toxins. All these things come together with thoughts, feelings, emotions, and beliefs to create your personal health status. Many variables are not within your control while others are. Identifying the healthful behaviors that you can control and modify while at the same time acknowledging that factors that you can't will help you make the most healthful choices you can.

• Eat healthy, fresh, nutritious foods.

• Move your body for strength, endurance, flexibility, and joy.

• Get sufficient rest and sleep.

• Avoid harmful substances such as tobacco.

• Use alcohol in moderation if at all.

• Keep up to date on routine immunizations and screenings.

All of these actions combine to maximize your healthy potential. You can awaken the healer in you with mindful meditations, visualization, and purposeful relaxation. Positive self-talk and a regular practice of self-nurturing guides you to being the most robust and disease resistant you can be.

Yet even in the best of circumstances we can become ill. Learning to know your body and be familiar with how well you feel is the first step to being able to notice when you are not well.

The health care system

The American health care system is a complex and enormous industry. When you or a family member is sick may not be the best time to learn to understand the way the system works. Your health and the health of your family depend on many factors, not the least of which is working with your health care providers. Here's how the health care system is organized.

Health care is a business, big business. And there is nothing wrong with a for-profit system. In a free capitalistic market, competition usually improves quality. Although health care supply and demand does not always conform to the normal market rules, it is important to look at the main players in the system so you can better understand how to participate in your own care.

Providers: The folks in the business include the providers of care such as doctors, dentist, nurses, dietitians, physical therapists, and pharmacists. There is also wide variety of allied health workers and alternative practitioners including naturopaths, chiropractors, massage therapists, and more.

Payers: Before WWII, people paid for their health care personally out of their pockets or care was provided for the poor by charity organizations and churches. Then, during WWII, there was a freeze in the labor market and the birth of the fringe benefit emerged. Health coverage for the poor and the disabled came about in 1965 with the passing of the Medicare and Medicaid act. Basically you pay for your health care either in the form of taxes or lost wages. Your employer or governmental agency buys insurance to cover the cost of providing care. Depending on how rich the policy is will determine the price of the premium. No care is free, nor should it be. Trouble happens when the financing of care gets too involved with the practice of medicine. Don't let this bureaucracy become a barrier when you seek care.

Collaboration is a partnership

Studies show that when people know more about their health, they make better health care decisions. Everyone agrees that we want affordable, high-quality health care that is easily accessible. Getting the right care from the right provider at the right time in the right setting is critical to our very lives. Learning how to use the system appropriately is really the key.

Together with your provider you can make the decisions that will work best for you in each circumstance. Today, people are more interested in understanding what is going on in their bodies. With the aging of the baby boomers we see an increase in the desire for information about our health and a demand for participation in health care decision-making. We are in an age of medical collaboration. Yet most of us do not have the skill or the language necessary to communicate effectively with our health care team. It is difficult to ask questions or understand complex information when you are sick, scared, or both. With the framework of PARTNER to Empower, you will find an easier way to gather and process information so that you can participate responsibly in your health care.

PARTNER to Empower ™

Remember these tips when making a health care decision. Use this guide to formulate questions for your doctor.

Physiology and pathology: What is happening in my body? Ask what part of your body is involved and what role does it play in your health. Ask the doctor to draw a picture of the procedure or problem. Find out if someone else (such as a nurse, therapist, or pharmacist) can help you understand the condition better.

One of the main barriers to patient-doctor communication is the language barrier. Doctors speak a very complicated language and use jargon and abbreviations or initials. You use jargon in your job, so you can see how easy it is to forget that others may not be able to understand what you are saying, even if you are saying it in the clearest manner you can.

To overcome the jargon barrier, be sure to ask your doctor what the words mean in simple English. For example:

• If the doctor says you have a negative Pap test result, you might ask if negative or positive is a good outcome.

• When the doctor orders an MRI, you might ask what exactly does MRI stand for?

• If the doctor indicates that you have a coronary occlusion, you might ask him or her to draw a picture of what that is.

Of special concern are elderly patients who are reluctant to ask questions. Many folks in that era were taught not to challenge authority. They believe that asking a doctor a question is tantamount to doubting his competency. Also, many patients believe that their doctor knows everything about them and that he or she is 100% familiar with the medical record. Certainly, your doctor may know a great deal about you, but it never hurts to remind the doctor of relevant information.

Attitude and approach: What type of doctor do you want? An autocrat who tells you exactly what to do? A democrat who will let others help make the decision? Or a collaborator who consults with you and makes decisions together?

Doctors are busy people. Their schedules have many interruptions from simple questions to full-blown medical emergencies. We all expect to wait in the doctor's office. I suppose this is why they call us "patients."

The time that providers have to spend with you is limited. Some studies indicate that the average doctor's visit is between 7 and 12 minutes. Additional research tells us that doctors interrupt their female patients somewhere between 17 and 42 seconds after they start to explain the reason for their office visit. Women tend to build **rapport** when speaking to the doctor. This wastes valuable time. Men tend to **report** symptoms more directly, which allows the provider more time to investigate the problem.

When we go to the doctor, even if it is for a routine checkup, we all have apprehensions. We think thoughts of self-doubt: "I think I feel okay, I sure hope they don't find anything wrong, I just heard about the gal who... blah, blah, blah." When you combine this nervousness with the awkwardness of waiting in a cool room without your clothes and sitting on paper, it is easy to see how hard it is to have an intelligent discussion. I recommend that you try to speak with your doctor before you have to undress. This way you can feel more comfortable while you are expressing your concerns and listening to the doctor's advice.

Reasons and risks: What are the risks associated with this decision and what is the likelihood that they will occur? There is always a risk with any medical procedure.

Treatment and tests: What are the tests for? Is there advance preparation you can/must do? What treatment options are available? Is watchful waiting a possibility?

Of greatest importance is to understand what will be done with the results of the test. Many times a test is performed to gather information upon which to make a decision. You should ask what decisions are pending.

Nutrition and lifestyle: What can you do in terms of nutrition? Here you must also consider lifestyle choices as part of a treatment plan. It is time to stop smoking, use alcohol in moderation, if at all, stay up to date on regular medical screening, wear sun block, manage stress, exercise regularly, and avoid exposure to harmful substances. You play a major role in your own health status.

You are already the expert in managing your health and health care. You know more about your body than anyone else. Furthermore, you care more about the outcome of any health care intervention. It's your body, ladies, and it's time to take charge. You already have many of the skills you will need to partner with your health care team.

Expense and emotions: Be aware that there is a price to pay for all medical treatment. Nothing is free. You have co-pays and the cost of your time and energy. Medical care decisions should be made in the best interest of your health, not because there is a third party payer. Appropriate utilization of health care services is best.

It is also important to consider the emotional costs of a medical procedure. Your time and stress are important considerations in the management of your health.

Research your options: Before you make a medical decision, be sure to get all the information you need. There are many good sources of information in bookstores, libraries, and on the Web. Be sure to use a trusted and reputable source that you can depend on for honest and accurate information.

Reviving the BEST in You:
CPR for the Spirit

Kay Ryan, RN, PhD

Kay Ryan is a registered nurse with a master's degree in health education and a PhD in community and human resources. Kay worked as a staff nurse in Critical Care for a number of years before pursuing her vocation in health promotion. Currently, Kay is Professor and Chairperson of Health Promotions at Nebraska Methodist College in Omaha, where she directs graduate and undergraduate health promotion educational programs, a holistic campus wellness program, and local, regional, and national community outreach.

Kay has been married to Jim for 31 years and is the mother of three: Jamie, Kara, and Kevin. She lives in the house where she grew up — in Omaha. Kay is passionate about her family and friends, her work, sand and water, and Irish music. Kay and her son Kevin spent the first academic semester of 2001 in Ireland. Kay plays the *bodhran* (Irish drum).

My Story

Do you constantly ask yourself if you know enough? If you are good enough? I have spent my whole life feeling as if I don't know enough and that I am not "good enough." I don't remember this feeling ever having a beginning. It's just the way I always was. I do remember that by the time I was a brand new graduate nurse, this had really become my primary way of thinking about myself.

I graduated from an excellent nursing program and was given several job offers right away. I initially chose a position in obstetrics. Although I was very well prepared academically and professionally, I was haunted by the idea that it was just a matter of time before everyone figured out my inner secret: I didn't know enough, I wasn't good enough.

I took every available opportunity to change this picture. I learned the latest in technology and practices. I collected certification after certification. I went back to school and earned additional degrees. I put myself to the test over and over again.

I managed to keep the "truth" of my inadequacy from everyone around me, while I continued to work and raise a family. My nametag and lab coat took on an ever-increasing armor of initials and pins signifying additional certifications and skills. In fact, I was a member of a critical care team that did a lot of great things and saved numerous lives. But I still waited for that inevitable moment when everyone would find out what I already knew: that I didn't know enough and I wasn't good enough.

About three years ago on a Friday afternoon, I received an urgent telephone call at work from my husband. Our 14- year-old son had been hit by a car while walking home from school. He had sustained a severe head injury and had been rushed to a trauma center. We weren't certain if Kevin was still alive. We were told to hurry.

I had cared for many victims of severe head injuries during my career in Critical Care. I began to take stock of everything I could remember about neurology, head injuries, the latest treatments, and especially outcomes. I knew it would be touch and go, at best. I was terrified.

I rushed to the Emergency Department and was taken to a treatment room. Kevin was alive, but the doctors weren't sure if he would ever wake up. After all that I had learned and all the many critically ill people I had cared for, it seemed so wrong that I could do nothing. I stood there completely helpless. My beautiful teenage son was lying on a bed in front of me. He was so badly hurt. Suddenly, all my fears had become a reality. I didn't know what to do to make a difference. I didn't know enough. At this most critical time, I wasn't good enough.

So, I did the only thing I knew how to do. I held my son's hand to my heart and I wouldn't let go. I said to him over and over again: "Kevin, can you hear me? Kevin, this is your mom, and I will stay right here with you. Kevin, please wake up."

Eventually, Kevin was taken to the Intensive Care Unit. I kept holding his hand to my heart, repeating, "Kevin, can you hear me? Kevin, PLEASE wake up." My worried husband said, "The kid has been through a lot. Maybe we should let him sleep." But I couldn't let go.

About 12 hours later, Kevin stirred. I asked him again, "Kevin, can you hear me?" And Kevin uttered an irritated, "YES."

"Do you know who this is?" I asked.

In a very distant, weakened voice Kevin said, "You're... my... mom."

All of a sudden, I understood that **it isn't how much you know that makes you good enough — it's how much you love. Life isn't about accomplishments. Life is about relationships.**

So if you have wondered what you need to do to feel as if you are good enough, know this: If you care enough to be your best, you are surely good enough. Carl Rogers called it being "fully human," and you cannot be more than that.

Each of us has extraordinary gifts and talents, but it takes opportunity (grace) to let them shine. The great thing about grace is that it keeps appearing over and over again until we are ready to be our true selves (to be "more than enough"). There are strategies for reviving the spirit and acting on grace — for being the best we can be. I call them CPR for the spirit.

Kay Ryan

Reviving the BEST in You:

CPR for the Spirit

The C's

Confidence

First, identify the basic issues that keep you from feeling as if you are good enough. The first issue is confidence. Confidence is something that other people just seem to be born with, but not those of us with these nagging self-doubts. Are some people born with confidence? Do those people remain confident all their lives? Probably not.

I would define confidence as a moving target. It begins with those early relationships that teach you to trust your own judgment. The bar is raised every time expectations are added and accomplishments are measured. Maybe some people don't care about measuring up as much as others, but I doubt that is really true. I think confidence is more an issue of whether people perceive themselves as able to measure up to expectations.

I have a friend who thinks she can fly (metaphorically speaking). I have observed her for years, trying to understand where she gets her confidence. I have noted two things about her: She has a mother who believes she can do anything and never stops telling her so. Moreover, she surrounds herself with positive, affirming friends who reinforce her mother's message. The really interesting thing about her is that now that she is a mother herself, she gives the same gift to her children. Her sons are turning out to be vibrant, confident children who believe they can do anything!

Culture

The cultures you create have a great deal to do with being the best you can be. The culture that you create at home is a great example of how you make a difference. Cultures should reflect your core values about what an optimum world looks like. Sometimes we overdo our part:

"The Bear Family is just waking up in the big forest. Baby Bear goes downstairs and sits in his small chair at the table. He looks into his small bowl, which is empty.

— 44 —

"Who's been eating my porridge?" he squeaks.
Papa Bear ambles to the table and sits in his big chair.
He looks into his big bowl and it too is empty.
"Who's been eating my porridge?" he roars.
Mama Bear puts her head through the serving hatch
from the kitchen and says:
"For Heaven's sake, how many times do we have to go
through this? It was Mama Bear who woke up at the
crack of dawn. It was Mama Bear who unloaded the dish-
washer from last night and put everything away. It was
Mama Bear who went out into the cold early morning air
and fetched the newspaper. It was Mama Bear who set the
table, put the cat out, cleaned the litter box, and filled the
cat's water and food dishes. And now that you have both
decided to come downstairs and grace me with your
presence — listen well because I am only going to say this
one more time — I haven't made the *@#! porridge yet!!!"

(Anonymous)

We are responsible for creating the cultures in which we live and work.

We have all been in work environments where no one could thrive. I once worked in a culture like that. It was generally expected that we would not be able to succeed at the work we were given, and that we would be berated in some way for even having tried. For some reason, we tolerated these norms for a long time and tried very hard to do the impossible. In retrospect, my colleagues and I feel that we stayed in this negative setting out of concern for each other, but now that we have all left, we can see beyond the unhealthy culture we shared.

When we left, the culture had to change because *we* were the culture. We allowed, or perhaps even created, a culture where people were not treated with respect. We did not demand the basic human courtesies to which everyone is entitled. We tolerated an abusive supervisor and we acted out of fear, not empowerment.

My former co-workers and I still get together to reminisce. I use the memories to reinforce the idea that I know what I *don't* want to do for a living. Most of you also know what you do want for a work environment. When you own your responsibility toward creating a nurturing environment where people can be their best, you are helping to make that environment good enough for you and everyone else. You are opening the doors for grace.

Kay Ryan

Creativity

You are wonderfully creative, each and every one of you. The major issue around creativity is not whether you have it, but how you use it to be the best you can be. Creative people are often called "dreamers." Goals are just dreams with deadlines. So, if you have dreams, you have goals. According to research findings, written goals are a predictor of financial success. Why not write down your dreams (a.k.a. goals), and test the research?

P.S. In terms of creativity, mistakes are a good thing. If you aren't making any mistakes, you simply are not trying hard enough! A creative person can take an "uh-oh!" and turn it into an "aha!"

Compassion

Are you compassionate? Most human beings are compassionate. In health care, I have witnessed thousands of acts of compassion by ordinary human beings in all kinds of ways. I have been surprised at how people in the most difficult personal situations have found something left within them to comfort or aid someone else who is suffering. People open their hearts when the opportunity presents itself. The compassion around us everyday is mind-boggling.

Maybe a tougher question is: Are you compassionate with yourself? Forgiveness is an act of compassion that you can give yourself. Forgiveness is being unconditionally accepting of your own humanity. It means letting yourself know that you are good enough without having to be perfect. Forgiving yourself is the ultimate act of compassion.

Courage

It takes tremendous courage to face the world with fear in our hearts, but that is what many of us do every day. Courage is the ability to face our fears. I have learned a lot about courage from a woman named Kathy.

Kathy faced the diagnosis of metastatic breast cancer in the middle of her graduate studies. She was a single mom with a very important and demanding job, and she had every right to quit school, quit work, and succumb to fear. But she didn't. Instead, she completed three courses of chemotherapy and her thesis at the

— 46 —

same time. She went on to deliver the graduation address at Commencement. She talked about the love she had for her class-mates, and the love they had shown her. She smiled knowingly as she recalled the scary things they had encountered in the name of learning and the thrill of victory as she looked around her on grad-uation day and realized that they had all faced their fears and won. She sighed as she recalled the many life-changing events she and her classmates had seen each other through, and she honored the bravery in all of them. She didn't see herself as unusual, except for the fact that she was blessed with so many friends and such wonderful support. She was very grateful for what she had learned from her unique life situation.

I salute the Kathys of the world, because they are models for all of us. They are the best they can be *because* of their circum-stances, not in spite of them.

The P's

Purpose

Researchers have identified four groups of individuals who experience remarkable health and longevity: nuns, orchestral conductors, Mormons, and women listed in *Who's Who*. What do they have in common besides excellent health and long lives? This is the question that is currently undergoing a great deal of longitu-dinal study, but it is interesting to speculate. Perhaps these people have found the "fountain of youth" in their commitment to purposeful life work. In other words, they do what they love and their health and lives are better for it.

Prayer

There is increasing evidence to relate positive health outcomes to the power of prayer. It seems that the "prayed for" do better, whether we are referring to cells in a lab experiment or to sick people. Another interesting finding about prayer has to do with the people who do the praying. There is a growing body of data to suggest that people who pray are happier and experience less anxiety and depression. There doesn't seem to be one right way to pray, but I have it on very good authority that women of strength do pray.

Kay Ryan

The R's

Recreation

Whatever happened to having fun? When did we start to embrace the idea that if it looks easy, feels pleasant, or tastes good it must be *bad* for us? I think there must have been a conspiracy to eradicate fun. I'm here to counteract the conspiracy and point out the obvious.

It's wonderful to laugh. We know it feels good. It's pretty easy, too. If you could taste laughter, it would taste like chocolate. I'm sure it's very good for you. Norman Cousins said laughter could control pain. He used it himself. We know that laughter affects the immune response, and we surely don't need a research study to show us what it does for relationships. Could you laugh more? Is it something you can change?

Relationship

People can bring out the best in us. Dr. Dean Ornish has made a very convincing case for the statement that our very survival is dependent on the healing power of love, intimacy, and relationships. He talks about the epidemic of loneliness and isolation that affects us as a society. We can look around us and see that he is right. We are a global community in relationship crisis. What can we do?

It seems as if we all have plenty of information about how to have great, fulfilling relationships, yet not many of us have more of them than we know what to do with. People are lonely even when they are surrounded by other people. Go figure.

Perhaps it would be wise to start at the beginning of this complex issue. Maybe loneliness starts from feeling as if you aren't good enough. Maybe it's not about having other people around but about not being able to be your own best friend. If you believe that there will be opportunities to be the best you can be (grace), then you need to accept that there is a *best you*, and that she will be good enough. There are some things you can't control, but your attitude toward yourself is not one of them. You can look upon yourself with kindness, if you choose to.

I hear compliments about how great people are all the time. You would probably be shocked and surprised at how valued you are if you would really listen to some of the good things other people are saying about you. Maybe you should.

On being good enough

Remember: It isn't how much you know that makes you good enough, it's how much you love. Life isn't about accomplishments, it's about relationships. These are the CPR strategies for reviving the spirit:

C = Confidence, Culture, Creativity, Compassion, and Courage

P = Purpose and Prayer

R = Recreation and Relationship

Pay attention to opportunity. Pay attention to grace. You are more than enough, *you are wonderful!*

Wisdom of the Everyday Yogi:
A Guide to Managing Chronic Illness
for Every-Body

Ada-Reva Franklin, RN, MSN, RYT

Nursing has been a part of Ada-Reva Franklin's life for as long as she can remember. Influenced by two close cousins and her oldest sister, all Boston University School of Nursing graduates, she enrolled to fulfill a legacy. She graduated from BU in 1986. In April 2001 she received a master's degree in nursing education from Clarkson College.

Ada-Reva has worked in child and adolescent psychiatry, substance abuse, women's health, and public health. In 1992 she created a non-diet approach to food issues and wrote an accompanying manuscript called *Playing with Fat*. She also developed a yoga-based program on parenting and health education for women offenders in a residential treatment program. As a public health nurse, she has worked with families suffering from many of life's indignities bringing heart and presence to her work.

As a certified and registered yoga teacher, Ada-Reva teaches yoga in a home-based studio and has developed a program that is suitable for all bodies regardless of disability or level of function. She volunteers for the National Multiple Sclerosis (MS) Society

Wisconsin Chapter and has been instrumental in creating classes for people with MS in Wisconsin. She presents at conferences, offers guidance in finding qualified yoga teachers, and offers specialized classes for people with MS.

As a professional storyteller and entertainer, she weaves story, song, guided imagery, humor, and play into her presentations. Her work speaks to a vast audience including health care practitioners and people living with chronic illness. She has painstaking credibility as both a nursing scientist and a certified yoga teacher. Her knowledge is born of research, education, and deep exploration of self — bridging a gap between nursing science and the art of healing. Like the research from which this work is born, she is unique.

Ada-Reva Franklin
The Franklin Health Institute
333 South Main St.
Columbus, WI 53925
adareva@internetwis.com

My Story

Ever wonder about those people who, even in the face of profound tragedy, somehow manage to lead a full, almost enchanted life. Well, I did too. So I studied the phenomenon. I conducted a qualitative study that explored the lives of people with Multiple Sclerosis who practice yoga. The people I studied took charge of their lives and became great self-healers. They used a wide range of alternative and self-care strategies to heal and be healthy. I realized after the study that I function in a similar way.

I have faced many of life's tragedies. The loss of a mother, rape, obesity, mental illness, teen pregnancy, divorce, single parenthood, and then the ultimate jolt — Multiple Sclerosis. One day I explored my own life story with a trusted friend and she said, "Yes, I know your story but I never think of you in that way. You are not a victim or a survivor, you are just you."

Our life stories are an enormous treasure. They bring to life clarity and understanding of the people we are now, ascending from whispers of who we once were. The earliest memory in my story was birthed in springtime. I was five. Many things happened that I truly believe contribute to my ability to heal from life's adversity.

I wrote a small, insignificant blip of a poem, born of the love of a child for her mother. The poem was called *My Little Marigold*

— inspired by a marigold I planted in a milk carton and gave my mom on Mother's Day. The town newspaper published it and a writing career was born.

Soon after, we went on a field trip from school to an abbey. The monks were so sweet. The essence of kindness filled the air. It was like taking a bubble bath in love. There were spring lambs at the abbey. I held one to my breast. The breath of newness in her musky coat filled me with awe.

The next day I stood on my porch waiting for my best friend, Sharon, to return from nursery school. Saltwater mist permeated my being. I drifted to the moment beyond where she and I first met. "I have known her forever" was the feeling that welled through the quivers of my young heart. In our friendship rested the truth and beauty of all that is right in the world.

In the midst of all this, my mother was suffering from major depression. Due to her own personal demons, she refused to see a psychiatrist. My sister, then a nursing student, suggested shock therapy, a treatment pre-dating most antidepressants. I was taken in tow to a basement shock therapy clinic. My siblings were out finding their own way in the world, and that world did not have room for a quirky five-year-old. On one visit a door was left open. When I saw a man with electrodes on his head, my thoughts turned to fear, "I must never show sadness like mommy, or someone might do that to me."

Then my grandfather died. He was a beautiful man with a thick head of soft gray hair smelling of wild earthy wind. I walked into the bedroom just as they pulled the sheet over his peaceful face, and my five-year-old heart held no fear. The thought, "He was just passing through," gave me great comfort.

Thus my life was born. At the tender age of five, I experienced the wonder of birth in a springtime lamb and a cherished poem. I discovered the true nature of death in the loss of my beloved grandfather. I felt the crushing weight of fear and the secreting away of one's emotions in the shock therapy clinic.

My tender young heart was profoundly hit with these distinct aspects of life. Bringing to light this simple life outlook: Tell the truth, tread gently, smile, and treat yourself as you would treat your very best friend regardless of the situation at hand. Life is a rare and precious gift.

The work I present to you is infused with joy, wisdom, humor, pathos, and an occasional free-fall. It chronicles life, my life, and the lives of the people I have met through my research, my career, and my travels. I relay simple messages about the heart of the everyday yogi directly from the heart of a storyteller.

The exercises included in this chapter teach us self-healing. We can then engage this healing process with others. The healing I discuss relates to body and breath awareness inherent in yoga. It also discusses the use of play, music, storytelling, and creativity to engender healing on multiple levels. The exercises show how to be present in your life and in your body.

My message is simple. We are all capable of self-healing on our own terms. This chapter helps health professionals and chronically ill people explore — through the yoga, storytelling, play, and creativity — what those terms are and how to take actions to facilitate them.

Wisdom of the Everyday Yogi

A Guide to Managing Chronic Illness for Every-Body

Everyday yogis are real people with honest yoga practices that accurately reflect who they are and promote gentle growth from that place of truthfulness. Some of these people identify themselves as yoga practitioners, some don't. All are a breathing testament to people who took personal responsibility for their healing and succeeded against all odds.

The program is simple. People explore the healing process through movement, breath, creativity, play, and the stories of others, thus facilitating self-healing on individual terms. They share one thing, the true desire to heal from pain and a willingness to look at alternative options such as yoga.

A program for anyone

This program could touch anyone who is suffering from physical or emotional illness and their caregivers. It is designed for everyone:

- People living with chronic illness or disability
- Anyone who loves someone who is suffering
- Aspiring yoga practitioners
- Health care professionals
- People seeking inspiration
- Yoga practitioners and teachers
- Storytellers of all kinds

From storytelling to yoga

When a story is told, three people are united: the person the story is about, the storyteller, and the listener. With yoga (meaning union), a practitioner seeks to unify the body, mind, and spirit so they live harmoniously as one. This union is a process of exploring into the heart and spirit.

Yoga encompasses eight limbs or paths. All paths lead to a deepening understanding of the self and of the divine. Yoga can be made accessible to anyone who wishes to know it, in an easy and thoughtful way. Yoga is also a path of knowledge in which research, science and ancient tradition unite.

An estimated 18 million Americans practice yoga. This number is projected to keep growing. Yoga and other complementary health choices are often recommended for chronic pain and illness. Pain and suffering is rampant in Western culture. Diagnoses of chronic and life-threatening illnesses such as cancer, MS, fibromyalgia, and heart disease are steady or rising. Those who are suffering need hope and guidance, from a practical and professional point of view.

Significant research shows that when people with chronic illness take an active role in their own health, they often have better outcomes.

Yoga and MS study

The results of my research study, entitled *The Life Experiences of People with MS who Practice Yoga,* show that people that are chronically ill practice yoga for the following reasons:

- Increasing body awareness
- Deepening their understanding of god
- Relaxation and stress reduction

A strong desire to take their healing into their own hands was demonstrated by:

- Strong motivators to change behaviors thereby minimizing disease outcome
- Creative world views
- Affirming life philosophies

Healing is not about gaining physical function lost to illness, although this can happen. If you lose an arm, it probably won't grow back, unless you have the magical blood of a starfish. Healing is more about having the courage to live the life you always dreamed but never felt was in your power. Healing is about serenity, strength, and growth. Healing with yoga offers the science of an ancient practice. Healing as an everyday yogi adds nursing science and care to the mix.

The Exercises

Stories of triumph in healing are accompanied by related exercises in this section. The exercises, taken from my work, evolve through the lifecycle.

One: What is your life telling you?

Jan's entire physical existence dissolved after an acute flare-up of relapsing remitting multiple sclerosis. Confined to a hospital bed, she could not see, speak, or swallow. She had a nose-to-stomach feeding tube, and her movement was confined to her fingers. But her spirit reigned over these bodily imperfections.

Her nurse chattered away, asking questions of all sorts about her new teddy bear and her life — unable to find the absurdity in asking questions of a woman with no ability to speak. Jan responded by bringing her fingers up to her nose rhythmically. "Stop trying to pull out your feeding tube," the nurse said each day. The speech therapist witnessed this interaction one day and smiled bringing her own fingertip to her nose. "She is not trying to pull out her feeding tube, she is saying you are funny in sign language."

It was by connecting with her soul from that deep place of pain that allowed Jan to connect with her nurse. Jan tells us that, at any point we feel disconnected, we can make a connection again. Her case is extreme and poignant. In using the only language available in her condition, she got her message through, and her soul survived intact. She tells the story with great gusto now that she is well on her way to recovery.

Exercise: Meditation on calling back your soul, a look at gestation.
Securing Sacred Space: Find a comfortable space on your bed or on the floor. Consider lighting a candle nearby and/or incense. Use a blanket if needed for warmth. Play gentle instrumental music if desired.
Body Position: Lie on your side in a fetal position, hips flexed, knees bent to a point of comfort for you. Place a cushion between your knees and a cushion under your head.

Breathing: Take full deep breaths through your nose, fill your belly with breath, fill the lung area, fill the area around your collarbone and exhale through your nose (or mouth).

Imagery: Have a friend read this to you or tape record it and play it to yourself once you are in position. Keep your focus on the full deep breath and the imagery. Close your eyes. Imagine you are floating in salt water, an ocean, a mineral bath, or a womb. You are buoyant yet immersed and breath flows freely. Allow yourself to float, unite the body/mind in the ways of spirit. Ask yourself, "What have I lost to illness, grief or pain, and what do I need to be whole again?" As those things occur in your mind, gently call back all that you lost. Allow yourself at this time to be whole yet again with what was lost. Connect to your breath and continue breathing through the process. When you are satisfied, float with the breath and, when you are ready, deepen the breath, open your eyes, and gently return to subtle gentle movement.

Two: The wisdom of pain

Sherry is a lively vivacious woman, wise yet vulnerable, strong yet fragile. Her husband died tragically a year ago, and the mourning process has been difficult. Her husband was her first boyfriend, her first love, her passion, and her heart since age 14. She mourns the loss of the love of her life but also mourns the loss of her youth and health to the crippling effects of fibromyalgia.

The face in her wedding pictures is that of a young slender Mary Tyler Moore. She had a brilliant singing voice. One wedding picture shows her singing to Ron, her new husband. She sang words of love eternal to a late 1950s beat. It was a marriage centered in love and passion, and it endured much.

On their 25th wedding anniversary they went to visit Graceland. Sherry was a lifelong Elvis fan. Singing and moving to his music was a great passion of hers. In the motel room she experienced a crushing stabbing pain throughout her back and spinal column. Ron just held her in his silent loving way.

The pain grew worse. It was often hard for her to move, yet she did what had to be done for her husband and family. Sherry worked two jobs when needed and lived her life. Ron held her with love and gentleness all the while.

When he died, she lost her one great true love. She also lost the man who helped her in her pain and anguish. A piece of her died too, for a while. There was no one who could hold and love her like Ron always did and that caused great anguish both physically and emotionally.

Six months after his death, her daughter Liz had a severe back injury after a motor vehicle accident. She sought the help of a gifted massage therapist and suggested Sherry might be helped as well. After one session Sherry felt much better and continues to seek treatment from the therapist. Sherry can tell you with great clarity how and why the therapy helps. She describes her muscles as being filled with junk and states that the massage frees up the junk from the muscles.

Yoga does that too. It cleanses the muscles, joints, and connective tissues of "junk" as Sherry puts it, allowing for greater ease in movement. Using breath and movement at your own pace, you can begin to heal as Sherry and Liz are now doing.

Exercise: The serendipity trail, a game of discovery.
Securing Sacred Space: Spread a blanket on the floor. Bring a pillow and any soft objects of comfort such as stuffed animals or favorite cushions. Survey your home for any objects that are sacred to you and arrange them artfully beside the blanket. Place a journal and pen by the objects as well. Play some music you consider playful or fun, use incense if desired. You may sit, lie, or stand, find your own place of comfort to begin your movement. Find others to do this with so you can share if desired.
Breathing: Breathe fully and deeply.
Imagery: Take a moment to examine your sacred objects, explore why they have meaning and then place them aside.
Movement: Begin with a still body, pace yourself to your music and begin to gently move your head as if shaking it "yes" up and down, then side to side. Roll your shoulders forward then back. Keeping the breath full and deep with each movement. Shrug your shoulders toward your ears, release them with a sigh. Raise your arms up overhead, circle your fingertips in the air, and lower the arms slowly to your side. Now from where you are, find your own movement and rhythm to the music. Gently stretching and releasing — sighing or moaning with your body for the duration of the music you selected. When the music has ended or a new song begins, use this time to rest with pillow, blanket, and toys before the game begins.

The Game: Take each object and write in your journal or tell to your neighbor what it means to you. Create a story from objects. Show an object. Spend a little time journaling about the experience.

Three: The uncharted waters of emotion

Mae was a lovely young woman in high school during the Depression. She lived in a religious Jewish home and felt her life was filled with the love of her god and the joys of friends and family.

One day she began to question her existence. At the kitchen sink while washing dinner dishes, she paused and asked god why she was put on this earth. Between the drips of water a silence ensued that pierced her soul. The swirls of dish soap and grease in the dishpan offered a pictorial to the deafening silence and out cried these words, in the voice of her father. "Mae, mine *claynekeh*, help already, the dishes must be done before bedtime." Help was the operative word. God had put her on this earth to help other people.

She finished the dishes and rushed out to tell everyone she knew that we are put on this earth to help others. She told Uncle Larry, Bubbah Mary, the Finkelman twins, and the Rabbi. When the Rabbi heard her message, he called for a family meeting.

Mae was brought belongings and all to see Dr. Kline. He worked at a big brick hospital across town. He asked her about what she was experiencing and she told him everything. The whole dripping-water, soap-scum, I'm-here-on-this-earth-to-help message. Dr. Kline had a suggestion, and he was sure her parents would agree. He suggested she stay there and help with his patients, there was much help to be done including dishes.

Sadly her parents said goodbye. She was given a room and a roommate and a dresser to put her things in. She worked tirelessly to help others. She bathed, fed, and dressed the people who lived there. She worked in the garden. Every night she took solace in her beloved dish soap scum.

One day a familiar face moved into the room next to hers. It was Minnie from her old neighborhood. Minnie wore the frown of someone who had sat on one too many pincushions.

"I heard you were here, Mae, what is this all about?" Minnie demanded with a scowl. Mae told her the whole soap scum story, about helping people. "Do you know where you are Mae?" Mae looked puzzled.

"I'm here in Dr. Kline's hospital to help, right?"

"You are not here to do any such thing, you are in the state insane asylum, Mae, and you are not the hired help."

Mae retreated, feeling betrayed by her family, her god, and her self. She became very depressed, a depression that took many years to relieve. She did succeed and in her success became the most incredible helper of all who knew and loved her. People thought she had the presence of an angel.

Exercise: Sitting in the corner with your feelings, a breathing technique for healing old wounds.

Securing Sacred Space and Body Position: Place a firm cushion, folded blanket, or meditation cushion on the floor by the wall or the corner. Pad your back with blankets or pillows so you are sitting upright yet supported by the wall or corner. You can sit cross-legged or support your legs with rolled blankets or towels. Be certain that you are comfortable and able to sink into the support. Light a candle or incense and play soft instrumental music if desired.

Breathing: Take full deep breaths through your nose, filling belly, lungs and collarbone area. Keep breath smooth and comfortable. Let exhale match the inhale.

Imagery and positioning: Close your eyes. Breathe as directed. Imagine you are sitting in a large clear bubble. The bubble is red and drifting in the wind. It floats up and turns orange. With each float up it changes color after orange is yellow, green, blue, and purple. The bubble is then permeated with soothing white light, which places you gently by a cool stream. Imagine how your stream looks both in vegetation and wildlife. The stream is magical and allows you to both pull up and let go of old feelings. Examine what you may be holding on to as well as what you are willing to let go of as you breathe deeply. When difficult feelings arise, breathe into them and watch to see if your breath transforms them. Anything you are done with can be put down the stream in whatever way you like (perhaps a Tom Sawyer-style raft). Be creative and allow things to drift or call them back if need be. Let go or hold on to whatever you like. When you are done, allow the white light to find you again. Sit back in your bubble and let it progress from purple, blue, green, yellow, orange, red. When you have landed again, be sure to keep your eyes closed for a moment and bring your body back with gentle movement.

Four: A bedtime story

Curl up with your blanket and pillow, light your favorite incense, and play gentle music. Let someone read this story to you:

Once upon a time on the wide Atlantic Ocean lived two children, a boy and a girl. They walked together to the beach every day after school and played until sunset. Huge sandcastles, sand angels, and seaweed mermaids were constructed. They were eight years old and totally in love with life and play and each other.

One night they both wished a secret wish upon a star that they would always be together, and they knew it would be true. They made a pact that if ever they lost touch with each other they would simply return to the beach. Innocent enough but life is funny. When eight turned to 10 and boys and girls were at odds with one another, the two parted ways and never played again.

Thirty years after the secret wish, each went to the same beach. Each brought an eight-year-old child in tow. They put on lotion and oil and sunscreen. They read their books and focused on their own world as the children found one another and played.

I now invite you to finish the story and start anew. Keep your breath even and love yourself as you do this.

Life can be cruel, difficult, joyous, uplifting, and sometimes seem a terrible hoax, but it is what it is. By finding our hearts in movement, breath, play, joy, and creativity, we can find our lives and renew again. Play a game. Tell a story. Be the butt of a joke and move on. Be inspired to be the amazing person that you are and live from the full depth of your heart, spirit, and body. Be inspired to always temper this with sound medical care and personal advocacy. Be inspired to use all of your resources.

Mindful Coaching:
A Process of Fulfillment

Billie Frances, MA

Billie Frances is a licensed Marriage and Family Therapist, a licensed spiritual counselor, and a trained personal and business coach. Her vision is to guide mindful change through inspiration and empowerment. She supports individuals, couples, families, and group members through her private practice in San Diego.

Billie is passionate about teaching. She founded Mindful Coaching Training for therapists, health care and other professionals to learn to be present with their clients in order to empower change. She created and facilitated communication courses and weight management seminars and taught classes on time management, financial freedom, and spiritual counseling. She is a graduate of the University of California — Santa Barbara and earned a master's degree in 1989 from the United States International University. Billie is a member of the California Association of Marriage and Family Therapists, the San Diego Professional Coaches Alliance, and is a consultant for business and community-based organizations. Teaching, training, and counseling have taught her the value of working with and learning from others — this book project is one more step in supporting her vision.

Billie Frances

Billie Frances, MA
Guiding Mindful Change
4003 Goldfinch St., Suite F
San Diego, CA 92103
(619) 297-7542
billiefrances@earthlink.net
www.guidingmindfulchange.com

My Story

"That's it!" I thought, as I waited in my car for a light to change. The guest on a radio interview program had just described how she taught and counseled people in ways that empowered them. And in that moment in 1986 I knew I was to become a Marriage and Family Therapist.

I didn't have any idea what it took to enroll in the master's program, how much time and money I needed to complete the training process, or how to market and manage a private practice. Nor did I understand how this new possibility and my work history would allow me to recapture my lifetime desire to teach. (I had already gathered enough business cards from varying enterprises to create a wall-sized collage without fulfilling this intention.) All this would be revealed later. That day in my car, I made up my mind: "I'm going for it!"

My enthusiasm was met with discouragement. "Therapists are a dime a dozen," Tom said. "There's one on every corner," Heather said. There were other personal and professional setbacks too. I had to repeat a course, which delayed my graduation a full year. There was a divorce fraught with betrayal and several failed attempts at the state licensing exam. My finances diminished after I traded home ownership for an education.

But desire to use my talents to reveal wholeness within others and myself proved stronger than these disappointments, failures, and financial insecurities. I stopped trying to figure out what the examiners wanted and gave them what I had. I stood by my authentic passion and released the outcome. Finally a miracle occurred. I received my Marriage and Family Therapist license in 1993.

My career in counseling provided the opportunity to support individuals, couples, and group members and gave me an opportunity to teach. Surrender had led me back to my passion. I created and facilitated couples' communication courses and weight management seminars and taught classes on financial freedom, time management, and spiritual counseling.

In 1996 I received training in personal coaching and four years later began teaching Mindful Coaching Training for therapists, health care providers, teachers and others who wanted to add the skills and methods of coaching to their profession. Creating and facilitating Mindful Coaching Training has delighted my heart and blessed my life.

Mindful Coaching is founded on the premise that beyond talent, opportunity, or perseverance we are inspired by deep passion and commitment. The purpose of mindful coaching is fulfillment. The vision is to develop a greater awareness of wholeness as foundation of all change.

Mindful Coaching is a process that encourages acceptance and guides exploration. Its questions invite us to be aware of our values, thoughts, and feelings as well as our circumstances and surroundings. Working with a coach and learning to be our own coach promotes powerful and transformational change.

In 2000, 14 years after hearing the radio interview that changed my life, I was approached to co-host *It's Your Call,* a radio talk show in which callers receive coaching on the air. The show is dedicated to helping people connect with their dreams and take action to manifest their deepest desires. I had come full circle.

In service to my clients, students, callers, and myself, I have come to understand that to teach is to empower.

Mindful Coaching:
A Process of Fulfillment

The process of fulfillment requires our undivided attention. Choosing a life on purpose rather than living an unexamined life means that we trust the moment and are present in it. To be present is to be mindful. Mindfulness is awareness. Mindfulness is recognizing our connectedness to all things. Mindfulness is making thoughtful decisions based on our inner wisdom from a deep understanding of our life's purpose. Mindfulness means being attentive, nonjudgmental and accepting. Mindfulness is the choice to live consciously and to let go of any desire to control, achieve, or resolve.

The process of fulfillment is ordered. Growth follows a natural progression. This is not to say that there is a straight line from where we are to where we want to be. The natural progression is that the land needs to be prepared before it is seeded, and a seed needs to be planted before the harvest. And as nutrients are added and weeds are removed, the seedling gets stronger. As we apply this analogy to our living including our desire to expand and grow, we discover ease in awareness and an abundant harvest by grace.

The process of fulfillment is its own reward. The joy of living the process is the awareness that there is nothing missing and nothing to do. We need not wait for the rose to be in full bloom to appreciate it. It is also magnificent as dormant potential.

The process of fulfillment can be learned and practiced. We may be more accustomed to answering urgent demands for our immediate attention than waiting, watching, and being in the present moment. We can learn to make thoughtful rather than snap decisions and heart-connected responses rather than off-the-cuff remarks. We can learn to be vulnerable rather than guarded and to be connected rather than cut off. We can rediscover the nobility of patience and renew our trust in the evolution of our lives.

Use the following sections to expand your personal and professional fulfillment. The process narrows from an all-inclusive ring of personal awareness to targeted goals and actions. Each section includes **Contemplation and discovery** questions to inspire the process of change. Spend as much time as you need with the questions. Some answers may be easily gathered while others will sprout over time. Be patient with your pace and with yourself. Coach yourself with compassion.

LOVING KINDNESS — clearing the land

Releasing discontent as the impetus for change is the first step to fulfillment. Change that is motivated by trying to make us better is rooted in frustration and fear. Mindful change approaches both what is and what we desire with kindness and awareness. Acceptance blesses where we are and asks that we completely approve of ourselves. As we learn to be present with who, what, and where we are and wish to be, we discover our next step is revealed with ease and by grace. Deep appreciation is how we best clear the way to fulfillment.

Contemplation and discovery:

* What is sacred about this moment?
* How can I be more peaceful right now?
* What am I grateful for?
* Which thoughts, physical sensations, or emotions need my attention?
* How can my mind, emotions, and body be in loving communication?
* What are my good intentions?
* How can I remember my joy?

MIND YOUR MIND — preparing the soil

Minding the mind requires vigilance. Our thoughts can lead us toward our heart's desire or burden our hearts with hopelessness. We need to be aware of our thoughts as soon as they sprout. Thoughts or beliefs that support our highest good, and harm no one, can be nurtured and blessed. When we notice thoughts that diminish others or ourselves, we can gently weed them out lest they overtake our positive intentions and choke off our good.

Just as we may need quiet in order to think, we need awareness in order to know our thoughts. Techniques to improve awareness include:

* Silent contemplation or meditation
* Keeping the company of others who are happy

- Journaling
- Taking time to appreciate nature
- Establishing order and balance
- Joyful movement
- Music
- Helping others
- Creative expression
- Prayer
- Laughter
- Expressing love

Mindful practices that completely capture our attention unite us in a very powerful way with others, our surroundings, and ourselves. We forget our separateness and remember our connectedness with all of life. While it may seem as though we lose ourselves in these practices, it is perhaps more accurate to say that we find ourselves as we surrender into them. Our souls sigh. Doubt and fear dissolve. We belong. Returning home in mindful connection, we release thinking and embrace knowing. Mindfulness guides and guards our fulfillment.

Contemplation and discovery:

- Which current beliefs support me? Which limit me?
- What do I need to forgive in others or myself?
- What could prevent me from succeeding?
- What do I need to release in order to make room for this?
- How does this serve the well-being of others and myself?
- What would it take to be present right now?
- To whom have I given my power?
- What are my assets?
- What makes me stand out?
- How do I make a difference?

VISION — dedicating the land

What do you wish to grow? Do you wish to grow a business, develop a talent, expand your knowledge, embrace a loved one, learn a skill, start a foundation, master a trade, create a work of art?

So often we begin with action rather than contemplation. We want to get into motion, sow some wild oats, work by the sweat of our brow, stir up some dust. We fill our planners and electronic calendars with unending tasks. We huff and we puff and exhaust ourselves in the belief that surely enough activity will give us what we want. Yet we discover that activity disconnected from vision is short-lived.

Vision is the life force that inspires transformation. Vision reveals the higher purpose served by our labors and gives us stamina.

Allow time to be still and know. Embrace inactivity in order to discover the grand plan that is right for fulfillment.

Contemplation and discovery:

- What is my purpose?
- What do I want to create? Or to grow?
- What is inspiring this?
- What does my inner wisdom say?
- How can I best use my energy?
- How is this in alignment with my highest good?
- How will this be of value to others and myself?
- What will ground me when the going gets tough?

VALUES — planting significance

When our actions are motivated by what we hold dear, we are empowered by congruence. We value what we say is important. Values help us achieve our potential. We choose values from among alternatives then prize them publicly. Values may include:

- Family
- Personal and professional development
- Leisure
- Money

- Achievement
- Privacy
- Companionship
- Surroundings
- Independence
- Leadership
- Security
- Helping others
- Religion or spirituality
- Self-expression
- Recognition

As we reflect on our values, we become more aware of ourselves as individuals with a choice about our destiny. Values give us the framework and freedom to choose specific endeavors, associations, and lifestyle that help us express that which is personally significant.

Contemplation and discovery:

- What is most important to me?
- Which endeavors express my values?
- How does my allocation of time and money honor my values?
- Which personal values am I honoring right now?
- How are my values and the values of my associates aligned?
- How will I know if my values have been compromised?
- What is my strategy to keep my values in the forefront?
- What am I tolerating in people or a situation that opposes what is important to me?
- How could my speech, lifestyle, and environment best reflect my values?
- How can I define my values in terms that are most meaningful to me?
- How could I be more in integrity with people, places, organizations, or institutions?

COMMITMENT — consecrating the earth

A commitment is our word of honor. A commitment is a statement of intention that is ongoing. Commitments, unlike goals, are not measured or quantified. An example of a commitment in the area of relationship might be: *I am committed to having a mate who adds love and joy to my life.* In the area of health, a commitment might be: *I am committed to having vibrant health and physical well-being.*

Commitment inspires courageous action on our own behalf. Compromising our integrity creates suffering and causes visible and invisible distress. When we act in opposition to our commitments, we may experience uneasiness or confusion. Perhaps the inability to concentrate or a gnawing feeling in the pit of our stomach gives us away. We can use these warning signals to draw ourselves back into alignment with who we say we are. We gain well-being, momentum, and confidence by honoring our commitments and keeping our word.

Contemplation and discovery:

- What am I committed to creating in the area of career? Finances? Health?

- What am I committed to creating in the area of intimate relationship? With family and friends? For personal and spiritual growth? In my physical surroundings? For fun and recreation?

- How can I best remain true to my commitments?

- What could happen to undermine my commitment?

GOALS — the seeds of desire

Although commitments define the quality and characteristics of our experience, goals define the quantity and time parameters of our experience. An example of a goal that is specific, measurable, and delineated by time might be "to increase annual income 20% by June 30" or "30 minutes of aerobic exercise, 3 times per week." Declaring how much, how many, and by when clarifies the action. Goal setting as a process provides the opportunity to assess our progress, reconfirm our intentions, and determine whether or not our actions will take us where we want to go. Be bold in setting goals. Be gentle in observing and correcting them.

Contemplation and discovery:

- Why is this goal important to me? Is it challenging enough? Is it exciting enough?
- What are the criteria for success?
- How is this goal in alignment with my values? With my commitments?
- By when do I want to receive or accomplish this?
- What are the steps I need to take?
- How will these action steps help me reach my goal?
- How will I finance this?
- How willing am I to be out of my comfort zone?
- What is my strategy to observe and correct my goals?

ACTION — a labor of love

Taking action means moving from the abstract to the concrete and from concept to form. Actions that are inspired by awareness are joyful, timely, easy, and fulfilling. Work that springs from clarity delights our senses with the sights, smells, and sounds of activity. Focus fortifies our intentions, unleashes our creativity, and enlivens our activity.

Contemplation and discovery:

- What needs to be done?
- What steps will I take?
- How can I best pace my activities?
- Do I have everything I need to begin?
- How will I overcome procrastination?
- What will help me stay motivated?
- What is most important? Most urgent?
- How can I break down the action?

SUPPORT — nutrients for the soil

The support of others is vital to our unfolding. We need people who will congratulate our attempts and our courage. We want to be acknowledged just for participating, showing up, giving it our best shot, risking, going for it. Comments, corrections, comparisons, or criticism are best delivered by invitation only and long after the workers have left the field. Sincere appreciation allows us to fulfill the purpose of relationships, which is to learn to love ourselves in the presence of another.

Receiving encouragement, working as a team, and benefiting from the collective wisdom are all worthy endeavors; however, asking for help can be precarious. We know that we are resourceful beings guided by inner wisdom, yet we desire to be in community sharing the common wisdom and multiplying our resources.

Somewhere between depending on others for happiness and isolating in search of self is a place where we are free to relate, share, express, enjoy, and celebrate with all in our homes, community, and world. There is a vast territory of possibility between dependence and independence. As we are willing to explore our options, and learn to release patterns of low esteem, we are free to step into healthy, interdependent relationships and partnerships. Interdependence is relying on each other in healthy, mutually beneficial ways. When we part company from separateness and come back to wholeness, we allow connection to nourish our souls and our endeavors.

Contemplation and discovery:

- How can I include others in ways that empower them?
- How could this be harmful?
- What or who needs to be acknowledged?
- Who else is or needs to be involved?
- Is there work I can delegate?
- Do I need to take time away to be alone with my thoughts and feelings?
- How will I know when to seek help?
- Would it be helpful to pray about this?

- Who can I humbly ask for help?
- How could I benefit from feedback?
- Have I given others and myself permission to make mistakes?

EVALUATION — surveying the garden

Evaluation takes place throughout the fulfillment process. Before beginning an endeavor of any kind, determine benchmarks for success and rewards for reaching them. During the activity, ask yourself questions to help you measure your growth and prune your activities. Make plans to reward yourself and others as you reach rest stops along the path of fulfillment.

Contemplation and discovery:

- How can I maintain balance with the rest of my life?
- How can I learn to observe and correct rather than criticize my action steps?
- How will I know if I'm on the right track?
- How well does my physical environment support me?
- What will keep me motivated?
- What are my tools for overcoming fear and procrastination?
- How will I respond to failure? To distractions? To setbacks?
- How can I reward my progress? Measure my results? Celebrate my success?

Mindful Practices — Essential Elements for Growth

Commitment is freedom. Practices done on a regular basis keep us on solid ground. Mindful practices are life-enhancing habits that nurture our physical, mental, intellectual, and spiritual well-being. Mindful practices expand our awareness so that we can increase our options. Secular routine becomes sacred ritual, and discipline generates freedom.

Give up the need to understand. We will naturally learn from our experience if we remain mindful and attentive. Through nonjudgmental discernment we become aware of what supports and what runs counter to our values, intentions, and well-being. Excessive time and energy spent analyzing, calculating, and assessing robs the creative process. Mindful observation allows us to correct our course. When we give up the need to understand, we open ourselves to knowing.

Everything is simply interesting. Nothing takes us out of the present moment faster than succumbing to specialness. When we believe that our result is the best or the worst or that we are completely amazing or completely inept, our comparisons return us to the past.

Interesting is neither faulty nor fabulous. Interesting is present-time awareness. What if we declare life interesting when events fall apart, interesting when events fall together, and interesting when life just is?

As we learn to simply observe rather than rate, all of our experiences become valuable. Rather than having ups and downs, try expanding the joy of now by accepting everything just as it is... *simply interesting.*

The soil is neutral. It simply produces according to the seeds we provide. Our role is to trust the creative process and nurture its unfolding. Our lot is to sow our passion and tend our garden with intention, awareness, and compassion. Our part is to weed out judgment, trim analysis, and harvest happiness. Our responsibility is to establish mindful practices to expand our awareness and enrich our lives. And our fulfillment is to embrace our wholeness, celebrate our connectedness, and abide in joyful unfolding.

One Damn Learning Experience After Another

Jennifer Hays, PhD

Jennifer Hays, PhD, is an Associate Professor and Director of the Center for Women's Health in the Department of Medicine at Baylor College of Medicine. She also directs the institution's Office of Health Promotion. Jennifer is nationally recognized for her research on the development of strategies to promote healthy lifestyles in women and children. She has published numerous scientific articles in the areas of weight control, the relationship between parenting strategies and children's health behaviors, and on risk-taking behavior in adolescents. She is the principal investigator of the Baylor Clinical Center of the Women's Health Initiative (WHI), the largest study ever funded by the federal government's National Institutes of Health on women's health, involving 164,000 women in the U.S. She serves on the eight-member, national Executive Committee of the WHI. She is also an Adjunct Associate Professor in the Department of Psychology at the University of Houston and is co-Director of the Baylor College of Medicine/Texas Woman's University Women's Leadership Institute.

Jennifer Hays

My Story

During the writing of this chapter, Hurricane Allison immersed my home in Houston with 8 inches of water, and if that weren't enough, I found my office at Baylor flooded as well. Thus the title.

One Damn Learning Experience after Another

Lesson #1: Loss

My first thought was "This can't be true. This cannot be really happening." It was 6 A.M., April 7, 1969. My father had just called me home from a slumber party and told me to go to my brother's room. I sat on the bed as he woke up my younger brother. Then he told us our mother had just died.

I should have seen it coming, but I didn't. My mother had been diagnosed with inflammatory carcinoma of the breast two years earlier, when I was 12. Her doctor had immediately sent her to specialists at M.D. Anderson Cancer Center in Houston, where she was told to put her affairs in order, that she had perhaps three to five months to live. But that was not what she told the rest of us.

She didn't believe it. She believed she could fight cancer and win. Her determination was legendary. She taught vacation Bible school every day that she received radiation treatment. She made jokes about carrying ammunition (BB pellets) in her prosthesis, which gave it the same weight as her other breast. When the cancer spread to her uterus, she pretended she wasn't alarmed. We pretended, too. When I overheard her telling my father that the cancer had spread to her brain, I heard her cry for the first time. He called his sister who came and cooked and made jokes and took her to her doctors' appointments and gave her shots for the pain that she couldn't ignore anymore.

On Saturday, April 5, we celebrated my mother's 42nd birthday. My aunt had gone home to spend the Easter weekend with her own family. Asking my mother for occasional help in reading her recipe, I baked her a birthday cake. My mother reclined on the sofa and friends came by to wish her happy birthday. Later I realized they had come to say goodbye. The next morning was Easter Sunday. I dressed in the red, white, and blue dress that we had fought about. I'd wanted the lavender one I'd seen on the cover of *Seventeen* that spring. My dad had finally pulled me aside and told me to let my mother have her way this time. Sunday morning she called me in to her room before I left for church. As I sat next to her and kissed her goodbye, she told me that I was the daughter she'd always wanted to have. Then she told me she had a sinus headache and to say hello to everyone at church. When I returned, she had gone to the hospital. She died early the next morning.

Lesson #2: More losses

My troubles were only beginning. A week after the funeral, my father told me that he was going to get married again. She had three children, and he was sure we would all be very happy together. Four months after my mother died, they were married, and we all moved into a larger house in a different neighborhood. I transferred to a different school my last year of junior high. My father had converted to a new religion when he remarried. Unfortunately, he decided at that point that my Sunday-School teaching mother had gone to hell because she wasn't of his new faith. Two years later he decided to quit his job and train for the ministry, so we moved to a different city where he could go to school. Within two years, I lost my mother, the father that I'd always known, my home, my friends, and all the caring adults — particularly my mother's friends, and my friends' mothers — who had stepped in after my mother's death to try and fill in for her.

Life at home became increasingly tense. I was not there very much. I was expected to buy all my own clothes, lunches, and school supplies, so I worked at several jobs in the evenings and weekends. I made tacos, I played the piano at a restaurant, I taught piano lessons. When I was at home, I studied. I began to throw up in the evenings. I was not bulimic (not that we would have known or used that term then). I wasn't intentionally trying to get rid of my dinner; I just couldn't keep it down.

Finally, a month before graduation, my father exploded when my stepmother found out I had gone to my boyfriend's house for lunch without permission. His mother liked me and often fed me when my money ran low. My father beat me with his belt and told me to be out of the house by the time he returned from a ministerial audition at a church in another state. So I packed my clothes and moved in with a friend. I left a note telling him where I was and informed the school of my change in address. My father changed his mind after he returned from his trip. He apologized and asked me to move back in. I decided not to. I was afraid that nothing had really changed. It would happen again. I thought that, if I left, things might get better for my brother. I continued to take him and my stepsister to school every morning so we could see each other at least for a few minutes a day.

Lifelines

Through all the difficulties I had at home, school was always a safe place. I did well academically and was the accompanist for an award-winning choir. But I didn't know what I was going to do about the future. A few weeks after I moved out, the school counselor called me to her office. She said that a Mr. Jackson who lived in a nearby town wanted me to call him. He was the father of one of my parent's oldest friends, my "uncle" Gene. Gene and his wife had heard from my aunt that I had left home and were worried about me. They sent a plane ticket to visit them, and I spent the next weekend describing what had happened to my brother and me since Mother died. They insisted that I come and live with them as soon as I graduated. They helped me find a job and apply for college. I worked and saved money that summer and fall and started college the next spring. I kept in touch with my brother, whose treatment at home continued to worsen. He left the following year without finishing high school.

I loved college. I threw myself into my classes and into the social scene. I worked part-time and was able to get some financial aid. My adopted parents sent me care packages of clothes and food and made me feel welcome on weekends and vacations. By placing out of a semester's worth of hours and going to summer school, I graduated in less than three years with a degree in psychology. I worked for another two and a half years before going back to graduate school. I liked graduate school even better than college. I enjoyed and was good at teaching, and the world of behavioral research opened up a whole new career path for me. I published several papers and gave scientific presentations at conferences. I fell in love and got married. I pretended I was normal. But I always felt different — that I was an orphan who really had no home or family.

You can run but you can't hide

Several years ago I read a column by Anna Quindlen in which she described how life-transforming and identity-changing it was for her to lose her mother while she was in college. She said that if she were meeting someone for the first time, she felt like describing herself as the brown-haired girl in the blue dress, the one whose mother was dead. I knew instantly what she meant. Losing my mother before I was grown made me feel like I was marked — like *it shows*.

For years, I thought I had come to terms with her death. My nature is to be optimistic, to find the silver lining. The summer after I left home, I remember driving down the freeway thinking, "There has to be a reason why I'm going through this. There must be a reason why I felt so loved and cherished for the first 14 years of my life, only to lose it so abruptly at that point. I must be in need of some lesson that this is teaching me." I noticed other mother-daughter relationships and decided I was better off having a great mother for a short time than an awful one for a long time. I practiced feeling gratitude for what I did have. But mostly I kept busy. I didn't want to feel how much I hurt.

I had learned from my mother that denying painful realities can be adaptive. Or maybe denial is genetic. But for 28 years I tried not to notice that I had a deep well of grief inside me. I became successful at my job. I wrote grant proposals and got research funded on health behavior. I did research on how mothers influence their children's health behavior. I taught and supervised graduate students in psychology. I coordinated health promotion activities for a large medical school. I had two beautiful children. My husband's mother and grandmother welcomed me into their family as one of their own. I discovered Judaism and felt as if I had found a way back to God after the painful experience of losing my faith in my adolescence.

My feelings of loss threatened to break through and consume me occasionally. Movies about mothers dying would do it. The pediatrician telling me that my mother would be there for me after my first child was born did it. But mostly I stayed busy and happy.

Until the day I outlived my mother. My mother had died two days after her 42nd birthday. As that day approached, I developed a plan to put a positive spin on that day. I sent luncheon invitations to seven girlfriends. On the cover was the poem, "Warning... when I am old I shall wear purple..." Inside, I invited them to join me in the wine room of my favorite Italian restaurant, to bring photos and stories of favorite old women, and to help me learn how to grow old outrageously. The luncheon was fun and inspiring. But I couldn't finesse the day as easily as I'd hoped. While I was in the shower that morning, the thought occurred to me that pretty soon I would find myself doing things that my mother had never lived long enough to do. Then it hit me like a blast of cold water: I had *already* done something my mother had never done. I'd gotten up that morning! I was still alive.

The bottom of the bottomless pit

The next few months were as difficult as any I've ever experienced. The expression "pay now or pay later" summarizes them. I found a good therapist who wisely realized that I had never allowed myself or been allowed to feel the loss of my mother and all the feelings that accompanied it. In her office I let myself fall into the bottomless pit of gut-wrenching grief that I'd been avoiding for decades. And of course it did have a bottom. In fact, I fell in several times, and each time I found the limits of my sadness and anger and emerged unharmed.

Then, the most amazing thing happened. By grieving for my mother, I got her back. Almost immediately after feeling the acute pain of losing her, her presence became almost palpable. One time, her words nearly knocked me off my chair. For years I could barely remember her voice. Now I can hear her voice in my head, commenting on a variety of people and situations. She was always a woman of strong opinions. I've learned to talk with her as one adult to another, rather than just be her passive child. I can argue with her when her voice is critical or unfair or uninformed. I've grown up.

I realize of course that she's been with me all along. I don't think it is a coincidence that I found myself doing research in health promotion and disease prevention. Or that I created a research center to study women's health. For the past five years, I have directed the Center for Women's Health at a major medical school. I am the principal investigator of Baylor Clinical Center of the Women's Health Initiative (WHI). The WHI is the largest study ever funded by the National Institutes of Health on women's health. There are more than 163,000 women enrolled in the study throughout the U.S., and we will follow them for at least 8 to 10 years. Some of the women are enrolled in a trial to determine whether eating a low-fat, high-fiber diet reduces the risk of breast cancer. The study is also investigating the long-term effects of hormone therapy on cardiovascular disease, osteoporosis, and memory. I look at the work that I have been a part of and I know that my mother would be proud.

I also realize that my life is not necessarily going to end early just because her life did. That I do indeed have the chance to do things my mother never did. When I first discovered this, I began to ask myself if I really wanted to be doing the things I was doing and living the way I was living. In some cases, the answer was no. I made some changes in the way I live. Many of them were painful and severe. I am no longer married. I have let go of several career goals that were more about climbing success ladders than doing meaningful work. I still say yes to too many requests and I am too busy, but I'm more discriminating. I seek friends and colleagues who are genuine and authentic. I think I'm more honest with myself. I am learning to love without hiding parts of myself.

I still believe that every experience is also a lesson. When we don't know the object of the lesson, we usually don't have a long or broad enough view. As I write this, I am temporarily homeless. While I was on a school trip with my daughter last month, the worst urban flood in the history of the United States deposited more than two feet of water in my neighborhood during the course of a few hours. My home was decimated. My office, which is in one of the most respected medical school hospitals in the world, is still without power and water one month later. The house is stripped to studs and slab and is slowly being rebuilt. My children are at their dad's house, I'm living with a friend, the dog is at my uncle's, and my furniture and possessions that survived the flood are in a warehouse somewhere across town.

I do not know yet what lessons I am learning from the flood. But I do know what lessons from previous experiences I'm applying. I know that blame is useless and a waste of time. That ultimately, we are all accountable for how we live — not necessarily for what happens to us, but how we take those events and use them. I know how to focus on getting things done. The only thing worse than a wet soggy carpet the day after a flood is wet soggy carpet a week after a flood. I know how to set priorities (life and relationships come before stuff) and use my resources. When friends called to help, I said yes, please, and thank you. I know to try and keep my perspective. I can find humor in the absurdity of government regulations and insurance vagaries. I know that I will be all right and that my children will be all right. I have survived worse and come out okay and I will this time too.

And again I feel like the girl who doesn't have a mother. Only this time, I can imagine my mother beside me, helping me sort through shoes, joking about Imelda Marcos' closet and offering opinions on how to redesign the kitchen (there are bright spots in every crisis). I will always be the girl whose mother died. But I'm also the strong woman who hauls a sofa out to the curb thinking, "I'm going to go with a different color scheme next time." I'm also the mother who can make sure my children know that a flood can only destroy sheetrock and wood—that our home is wherever we are together. I'm the researcher who gets conference calls at Starbucks and email wherever there's a phone line. I'm my mother's daughter.

And I wonder what the next lesson will be....

A Relationship Tested:
What Doesn't Kill You Makes You Stronger

Rande Davis Gedaliah

With over two decades' experience in help-wanted advertising, Rande Davis Gedaliah was founder and principal of her own
award-winning $22-million agency. In 1992, she partnered with her
husband, Robert, in *gedaliah communications,* creating,
marketing and implementing presentation skills and relationship
programs to meet the needs of an increasingly diverse corporate
community. Her focus is on gender differences in presentation style,
image, and verbal and nonverbal communication.

Rande is active in the National Speakers Association and
Toastmasters International (she's the Toast-Mentoring Chair for 180
clubs in the New York area). Robert and Rande have coached several
speakers who have competed in the Toastmasters International
World Championship of Speaking (including first, second, and third
place finishers!).

Established in 1984, *gedaliah communications* works with
people who want to boost their professional impact by developing
powerful communication skills. Through keynotes, coaching, and
workshops, they're a valued resource for many multi-national

companies, as well as individual executives and professional speakers. Customized programs include *Speaking for Results*® and *How to Communicate with Your Mate without Killing Each Other*SM.

Rande Davis Gedaliah
gedaliah communications
R@SpeakingForResults.com
www.SpeakingForResults.com

A Relationship Tested:
What Doesn't Kill You Makes You Stronger

Unlike a sailing-ship, a relation-ship might sink if the waters are always calm. Turbulence and rough seas test the seaworthiness of your togetherness. If you successfully weather the storms, there's a good possibility you could come out stronger…both as individuals and as a couple.

"Once upon a time…"

…when I was four years old, I awoke one winter holiday morning in a magical land! My parents had transformed our tiny Brooklyn apartment into a vision of glittering red cellophane. It was a moment that left me breathless with awe and will forever remain indelibly etched in my treasure trove of happy childhood memories.

The centerpiece of this rosy world was a beautiful doll nestled in a miniature baby carriage. I immediately named her Suzy and needed no encouragement to fantasize she was my very own baby. My mother had made matching outfits for Suzy out of the scraps of material from the clothes she'd sewn for me. From the instant I saw her, we were inseparable.

Most of us were taught, as little girls, to expect a perfect, romantic future. We'll be beautiful, fall in love with a prince just like daddy, get married, have babies…and live happily ever after. Those of us lucky enough to grow up in a loving home were shown, by example, how wonderful life could be for us as women and mothers.

Robert Gedaliah and I married in 1983, after living together for five years. We certainly married because we loved each other and wanted to build a future together. But we also wanted to start a family. It was time. Actually, Robert wanted a child even more than I did. He yearned to feel and give unconditional love and deeply wanted to be a dad. Not that we both didn't have some ambivalence, misgivings, fears…there was just never a question we would create a child. We totally bought into the romantic formula that love plus marriage equals children.

Both sets of parents and my grandparents were thrilled. They longed to have a grandchild to dote upon and spoil. The pressure from them was unspoken but definitely there. Intellectually, we knew we were the only ones who could choose to have a child or not, but we felt their excited anticipation nevertheless.

So, in 1985, when I was 37 and Robert was 40, we stopped all birth control and set about making a baby. We followed all the "rules." I quit smoking, cut out alcohol, started a rigorous exercise routine, and took my basal temperature every day. There was never a doubt that, with hard work and determination, nothing would deter us from our goal.

Every new parent is a parent for the first time. And everyone carries around a lifetime of emotional baggage. We have the choice of continuing to carry it, or find a way to lighten our load.

Plus, the decision to bring another life into the world ratchets up the intensity of any relationship. It's at this point the level of commitment to each other gets seriously tested, much like looking at ourselves in a big magnifying mirror. It is perhaps the most momentous, irrevocable, and scary decision a couple may ever have to make.

We thought we'd worked out the basics of living together and fooled ourselves into believing we were communicating in a healthy, supportive, constructive way. So to give our yet-to-be-conceived child a running start in life, we simultaneously began couple therapy with a wonderful, sensitive woman who also had chosen to have a baby late in life, while she was in her early 40s. We asked her to help us to be the best possible parents.

We didn't realize it at the time, but our therapist, Dr. Edie Cadenhead, was about to save our marriage.

The first neon sign of trouble was when we started fighting about what our baby's last name should be! I had kept my maiden name and wanted to give our child both of our last names (either my name as a middle name, or hyphenated with Robert's last name). Robert dug his heels in and adamantly refused. His reasoning? He didn't want anyone thinking our child was alphabetically a *Davis* and not a *Gedaliah!*

More ego fights. Fights about whose dead relative would become the baby's Jewish namesake. About which one of us would be the stay-at-home parent. About needing and not getting emotional support (we were both pretty vulnerable and needy). And, of course, about money.

We were unhappy, angry, and tense with each other, which certainly didn't support the baby-making process. Would you be eager to jump into bed (on a schedule, no less!) with the person who's the focus of your upset?

Meanwhile, Robert's brother and his wife gave birth to their first child, Jonathan. I was so conflicted! Most of me was flooded with joy to have this beautiful, perfect nephew to love, yet part of me was wracked with envy. Why not us? Why weren't we getting pregnant? We were doing everything right! It wasn't fair! We were so intent on making a baby, we forgot about making love.

As I menstruated month after month, year after year, we knew something was very wrong. I had been telling my body "no" for so long, we reasoned it would just take some time for the "yes" message to get through. We went to half a dozen infertility specialists, and each one would discover yet another roadblock.

I was allergic to Robert's sperm. My body would literally murder those little guys so there wasn't a trace of his sperm in my body during the post-coital tests. In turn, Robert developed an allergic reaction to me and broke out in an uncomfortable genital rash. After one particularly painful diagnostic procedure, it was determined my fallopian tubes were solidly gelatinous — totally and irreparably useless. "100% non-patent," the doctor told me in an uncaring monotone, while I doubled over in agony.

And there were other difficulties. Robert had "the three low Ms:" low motility, low morphology, and low mobility. In other words, his sperm were not strong enough to make me pregnant, so he had to be medicated for several months.

During this period, Robert spent a lot of time with titillating magazines in his urologist's office! One test was to see if he could make a hamster pregnant. (By the way, he now has a teenage rodent somewhere out there!)

Ultimately, our doctor said we might be good candidates for in-vitro fertilization. At the time, this was still an unproven experimental procedure. But it was our last hope. We were now in our 40s and had agreed this would be it. No more extraordinary means to have a child. We had put everything else in our lives on hold for far too long. The idea of adoption was discussed and dismissed. Because of our ages, we had resolved not to go through what might be a prolonged and aggravating process.

A few months into the IVF program at Mt. Sinai Hospital in New York City, one doctor was flabbergasted to discover what should have been checked years before: I could never have sustained a pregnancy in the first place! My mother had unwittingly been given the drug DES while pregnant with me, and I now had the classic symptom of a T-shaped uterus. After all those years of birth control pills, condoms, and diaphragms, all those drugs to become pregnant, all those infertility doctors, all that anguish, and I was incapable of ever giving birth!

Throughout these years, our therapist, Edie, would counsel us on our relationship. She'd say, "Don't you know you two have paradise?" Oh, the guilt I felt at not being able to make Robert a father. He should have married someone else, someone younger and "whole" who would make him happy, make him a father. And the resentment and frustration Robert was going through but couldn't verbalize without exploding.

It was a very tough five years. But we lived through it and it made us stronger. When our heads were clearer, we reminded ourselves our relationship wasn't about having a child, it was about having a relationship.

Unbeknownst to us, at the same time Edie Cadenhead was teaching us to function at a higher and healthier level, she was dying of cancer. What a magnificent woman she was. Sadly, her body was betraying her while she was giving us (and others) so much of herself.

A few years later, Robert and I were lying on a beach on the island of Anguilla. Under the warm Caribbean sun, this amazing peace washed over me! We weren't childless. We were childfree. Free to indulge in and concentrate on each other. Free to vacate when we chose. Free to travel together. What a mind-bending epiphany!

And, in a way, we do have a child: Our relationship is our child. That day, we promised to raise it as the best parents we could be, give it a good education, nurture and love it, so we might send our relationship-child into the world as an example of possibilities.

So, no matter if you are struggling with infertility, or have chosen not to have children, or even if you are already blessed with offspring, make the decision to make your relationship another child to love. As little girls, we believe in "happily ever after." But whose dreams are they really? We can always rewrite and re-rewrite our dreams and actualize our own "happily ever after," not someone else's idea of what our life is supposed to look like. Robert and I have made Edie's legacy a reality. We have lots of kids in our lives, including a spunky handful of a goddaughter, appropriately named Rocki. We're a lucky family, he and I. We really do have paradise.

Paradise — lost and found

Not being able to have a child was a wrenching disappointment. It almost destroyed our relationship. But setbacks also create opportunity for growth and change, like a phoenix rising from its own ashes.

Along with two partners, I was a founding principal of a $22-million, award-winning help-wanted advertising agency. Our company, Davis & Dorand, had 50 employees and three offices. Headquartered in the Empire State Building, we had branch offices in Beverly Hills and San Jose, California.

For years, I'd been working about 70 hours a week. By the time I got home, Robert was usually in bed, most times fast asleep. We saw each other on weekends — that is, when we both weren't on the road.

After 21 years in the industry, I wasn't enjoying myself anymore. I'd become an administrator. Our staff was doing almost everything I liked to do. My partners and I weren't getting along.

But we were making a lot of money. The proverbial golden handcuffs.

Then, in October 1987, the bottom dropped out of the stock market. Our client companies weren't hiring. They were laying off employees. We struggled to expand our client base just to stay afloat. Clients who used to pay their bills before the ink was dry were now taking 180 days or more to send payment. We were strapped for working capital. My partners and I put all our personal savings back into the business.

Then came the Gulf War. Young men and women volunteered to fight for their country in Desert Storm, and the companies for whom they worked decided not to replace them. Among his other cruel acts, Saddam Hussein hastened the death of our business!

Davis & Dorand shut its doors on March 22, 1991. What clients we could salvage we merged with another recruitment advertising agency, along with our entire staff. A dozen or more creditors were suing us, but there was no money.

Five months later, the car I was driving collided with a construction truck. The truck won. My spine was badly damaged. Now I was crippled and in excruciating pain. The day after my accident, my father had a heart attack. Thank goodness he's fine today, but it definitely added to our already high stress level.

Then, on Friday the 13th of December, two days after my spinal surgery, the phone next to my hospital bed roused me from a drugged sleep. Jody, my business partner, called to say the agency we had merged with a short 10 months before had declared bankruptcy! They had given us just two hours to clear out our desks before the marshals came to padlock the doors! Robert and my dad scrambled to grab as many of my business files and as much of my personal property as they could.

So here we were, with absolutely no savings, facing a long, painful recuperation, out of work, ducking law suits, and living on unemployment insurance, plus a modest income from my husband's business.

Robert had started his own communications consulting firm in 1984, offering speeches, coaching, and presentation skills workshops to the corporate community. He'd been asking me to join him in *gedaliah communications,* for years, but I didn't think it was a healthy idea for couples to work together.

Ironically, because I was now "between successes," I was able, for the very first time, to see Robert deliver a keynote speech! It was at a finance and technology conference for Lipton Tea. As I stood in the back of the room watching Robert on stage, I was blown away! He was really good! That's when it hit me: Robert's a creative spirit, a terrific speaker, but definitely not a businessman. That's what I could bring to *gedaliah communications.* Plus, I thought we could keep each other accountable and motivated. Robert had been doing all right in business, but he never felt the urgency to press harder. I'd been making enough for the two of us for a number of years. Since we didn't have children and could afford the risk of a single income, we decided to join forces — and almost killed each other because of our differences!

Robert micro-managed me to death! Here I'd run a $22-million company, and he didn't trust me to write a letter without breathing down my neck. He monitored my phone conversations with clients. Even followed me into the bathroom with the portable phone, for me to handle a client's call!

Robert was a mental popcorn-maker: He would come up with ideas almost as fast as he could say them. And I was so focused on details, I couldn't see beyond handling the project in front of me.

We were faced with a choice: We could each let go a little, determine parameters, and grow our business, or stay friends and go our separate career ways. First, we designated some rooms as absolutely, positively "off limits" to discuss business. No business or business papers in the bedroom or bathroom! Otherwise, our work would not only take over our lives, but our home, as well.

Then, we decided which of us was better at organization, sales, marketing, follow-up, delivery, and creating and designing materials and programs. The areas that continue to test our relationship the most are those where our skills overlap. We needed to trust each other to do what each of us does best. If both of us were deficient in an area, we subcontracted it to someone else. The realization that "it's nothing personal, it's only business" saved us! The value we embody is to make the needs of our relationship the most important thing in our lives. In other words: change "ego" to "we go." We learned to celebrate our differences and not censor each other. Opposite opinions and personalities work best when we don't make them personal issues. If we agreed on everything, there need only be one of us. There are certain things we can control and other things that are just way outside our ability to "fix." After a period of feeling impotent and "why us," we realized it really wasn't the end of the world. Actually, just the opposite!

Destruction created the opportunity for change. The five years of trying to have a child, culminating with the events of 1991, may have overwhelmed us for awhile, but it was an important lesson in the power of rebirth, regrowth, and reinvention. We rose from the ashes, much stronger, much wiser, and much closer as a couple — a family. We haven't "solved" our lives; we're still in transition. And the process of change is now more fun than pain.

A half-century later, my doll Suzy sits on a bedroom windowsill. Her clothes are long gone. Otherwise, she's in perfect condition. It took years to let go of those improbable childhood expectations and see Suzy as just a doll, as a happy symbol of what was, rather than the sadness of what might have been.

In summary, be *great-ful* for your relationship.

* Being *great-ful* is being full of greatness. Your relationship can be a terrific opportunity for personal fulfillment, if you let it become an ongoing process of self-discovery. It's someone to fight with and someone to fight for. No one can make you happier, or angrier.

- There's a difference between being competitive (which can make you stronger) and being rivals. Your mate is not your sibling! Play to win, not to hurt.

- One big misconception about a relationship is, in order to have a good one, you must have much in common. Not true! There is no such thing as one all-encompassing love. Embrace the areas you do share, overlook (or accept) what you don't. Try not to force your mate to adopt your point of view.

- Most problems in a relationship cannot be solved! Men and women are just too different. Given our impossible, romantic expectations, it's amazing we're able to have relationships at all! Learn to have a sense of humor about your differences and not take it all so seriously. (This might be put in the "easier said than done" category!)

- It's passion that pulls you together, but it's adversity that binds you together. How you handle the inevitable challenges will make you even stronger as a couple.

- A relationship is a mirror. When you look at yourself through your mate's eyes, can you see the person he or she sees? Do you like yourself better because of who you are together?

- According to the theologian, Dr. Paul Tillich, "the first lesson of love is to listen." Acknowledge, recognize, praise and, most of all, listen to each other. Your relationship will thrive on good, open communication. It's a priceless gift to have a supportive person in your life with whom to sound out ideas.

- And finally, "loving" is different than "liking." Even the most loving couple will occasionally hate each other. That's okay, as long as you've made your bond stronger than the damage you'll do to it. Remind yourselves often of why you like your mate. Savor all the moments, even the rough patches, for how you handle them will reflect who you are together.

- Be great-ful for what you have, who you are, and who you are becoming — separately and together — in like and in love.

Lessons Learned from Dolphins

Winalee Zeeb

Winalee Zeeb thrives on sharing the joy of movement and philosophies for balance and wellness with others. Teaching fitness classes since 1981, Winalee actively and eagerly shares body-mind wellness. She and her husband own and operate a scuba business in Lansing, Mich., and Winalee is president and owner of her own business called Heartdance. She holds a BA from Michigan State University and teaching certifications that include Nia First Degree Black Belt, Nia White Belt Trainer, Yoga for Health Instructor, Aquatic Exercise Instructor, American Council on Exercise Fitness Instructor, and Scuba Schools International Scuba Instructor. Winalee actively presents playshops and speaks at national and international health and fitness conferences.

Winalee Zeeb
Heartdance
(517) 372-3039
RWZEEB@aol.com

My Story

Legends of dolphin magic abound. Do they really happen?

Ever since I was a child, I always felt more comfortable and at home in the water environment than on land. In my story, I share how the dolphins helped me to embody living joyfully on land, experiencing community and connection awareness, as the dolphins model it, in my everyday life. These dolphin encounters remind me of simple life truths, which can inspire hearts and remind us all to live life fully and joyfully.

I have a poster in my office that reads, "To live on the land, we must learn from the sea." One of my loving sisters gave it to me many years ago, and I look at it every day. My friends in the sea have gifted me abundantly with tools that empower me to remember how to live joyfully on land. Sharing our story is my gift to you, dear reader.

I believe, as the Native American Indians teach with story-telling, that whether or not you are a water lover, or attracted to dolphins, the lessons I share here will be clearly felt and understood by your heart because they are universal life lessons. Your journey may have presented you with similar opportunities in different environments — perhaps in the woods or in the air. Regardless of the element you most comfortably resonate with, the message remains the same. I invite you now to allow your imagination to travel with me to the amazing and magical world of the sea.

Lessons Learned from Dolphins

Wet beginnings

When I was a little girl, I loved swimming underwater. In fact, I stayed underwater for such extended periods of time that my family would sometimes express concern for my well-being. One of my sisters even dove in to rescue me once, thinking I was drowning when I was simply enjoying my freedom underwater. The water environment has always been a home to me — safe, nurturing, familiar, peaceful, tranquil — a place where I feel most alive.

I was a shy child. I always felt "different" but had no idea why. Whenever I met strangers, I would automatically withdraw. If pushed to socialize, I would often run away in tears. I was happiest in the water or hugging my loving family and friends. My fondness for touch and hugging has carried over into my adult life, where my reputation as a "hugger" often precedes me. I believe these qualities of deep family bonds and my love of nurturing touch synchronize with my affinity with the dolphins because they are known for these same characteristics.

My passion for the water eventually led me to scuba certification and my marriage partner, Ron Zeeb — loving teacher, spouse and partner in our scuba business. Along the way, I began teaching water exercise at our local community college. Although I didn't have any official training in aquatic exercise, my classes were fueled by my enthusiasm and energy. That was the beginning of my journey as a teacher, one that continues today.

Taking a leadership role eventually healed me of my shyness, nurturing the actor and extrovert within. As I grew, doors began to fly open. I taught larger and larger groups and began presenting at conferences. Eventually, I took on the role of *speaker!* Never in my life would I have dreamed I would be standing before large groups of live bodies speaking from my heart in comfort! What a fascinating shift! Please know that these giant steps did not occur without fear. Fortunately, my teachers were always reassuring me to take a leap of faith. I am eternally thankful to all of them.

Winalee Zeeb

Just breathe!

In our scuba business, Ron and I are blessed with the opportunity to lead group trips, often to remote diving destinations all across the globe, because those are the places we prefer. These excursions have given me unlimited opportunities for marine life encounters — up close and personal. This story begins with my wake-up call — the experience that truly enabled me to be awake to later receive messages from the dolphins.

We were leading a group to the island of Roatan, located off the coast of Honduras in the Caribbean Sea. A huge tropical storm from the north had just passed through bringing with it Portuguese men-of-war (poisonous jellyfish), which are rarely seen in the area. The dive guides warned us to be on the lookout for them whenever we were on the surface of the water.

The very first day, I was making sure our group was safely back aboard our dive boat. I was the last one to surface. Just as I reached up for the dive ladder, Whhhhhhhhhhhhiiiiiiiiipppppppppp! I felt the excruciating pain of the swat from a stray man-of-war tentacle across my hand. I was not wearing gloves in warm water, so the tentacle struck my bare skin. "I've been hit!" I yelled. The group sprang into action and had my wet suit and rings off in moments.

I immediately observed myself having an allergic reaction to the sting. There was no hospital on the island, but they had an EMT station, operated by a missionary, where I sat on a gurney just five minutes after the hit. I witnessed myself not breathing and could overhear them saying they did not have anything to give me — no adrenaline in the house — and that they would have to air evac me to Honduras.

I began experiencing anaphylactic shock from the venom. I felt as if I were watching myself from above. I became aware that I wasn't breathing. My angel, Shirley Ritter, a loving long-time friend, was holding me, whispering the mantra in my ear, "You're alright, Winalee, you know you're alright." As I looked down from above, Shirley's words became louder and the words of panic all around me grew softer. Suddenly I sat up and began breathing with forceful exhalations. Within a minute my convulsions had stopped and I was back.

The wake-up call, my lesson from this encounter was, "JUST BREATHE!!!" I am so grateful to that stray man-of-war tentacle for reminding me of the importance of the gift of life, of spirit, of *prana*, of *chi*...**breath!!** — a powerful healing tool. That day "happened" to be my birthday and I now celebrate it as my "birthday" in multiple ways.

Lighten up

Now enter our dolphin teachers. Our first fabulous wild dolphin trip was with a group of close friends in the Bahamas' Outer Banks aboard the *Dream Too* live-aboard dive boat. When seeking wild dolphin swimming encounters, you're much more likely to have success if you travel with people familiar with the resident pods' activities and behavior.

I learned a lot from our captain and guide Scott Smith about honoring the dolphins' personal space by swimming beside them and not directly at them or chasing after them. We all know who the better swimmer would be. He taught us that if the dolphins grow to trust you, they will let you know if they're interested by getting closer to you. Sometimes they invite human touch by swimming even closer.

I learned the importance of simply creating the space, letting go of any agenda toward the final outcome of each snorkeling experience, to be in the moment and enjoy the ride! All of these encounter tips I find so true in any relationship — trust, surrender, acceptance, and presence. Ahhhhh! Thank you, dolphins.

On one glorious swim with a pod of approximately one dozen female Atlantic Spotted Dolphins and their babies, Paw Paw, one of the moms, and her baby, Darby, spiraled away from the pod and swam toward me. (Scott is so familiar with this pod, he has named them.) I was submerged at the time, doing what is called breath-hold diving with mask, snorkel, and fins. Suddenly baby Darby swam into my space pausing directly in front of me.

Looking into his eyes, I felt his limitless love piercing my being. As I was mesmerized by this momentary, yet timeless experience, I received my first message loud and clear: "LIGHTEN UP!!!!!" This is a message I *needed* to hear. I was smiling and beaming with joy as I gently reached out my hand to stroke Darby's silky skin. He stayed and allowed me to give him love in return for what I received as mom watched from nearby, obviously trusting me as well.

Wow! What an honor! What an amazing gift. I had just been given my first encounter and it was with a baby — they are very protected by the pod. I was forever changed in that moment. Whenever I get stuck in my "stuff," Darby's message reminds me to "lighten up" and not take things so seriously. Power resides in simple truths.

In my daily life, I am constantly reminding myself to breathe, embrace the moment, trust others and myself, accept life as it unfolds, create space for my intentions, surrender to my need to control outcomes, and especially to lighten up and play more. Sometimes I forget. Then I remember the dolphins and am reminded again.

We are one

During our repeat trip the following year with our friends aboard the *Dream Too* in the Bahamas, I was blessed with another life-enhancing dolphin encounter.

We had been snorkeling with a pod of spotted dolphins, having a fabulously joyful time. As I was surface diving beside the pod, I was feeling totally giddy and childlike. Swimming playfully with a dolphin-like kick of my fins, I enthusiastically attempted to imitate the real pros that were displaying their graceful glides before my eyes. My heart was full of love and I had no intention of touching the dolphins or of attempting to physically get closer to them.

I was totally immersed in the joy of the moment when suddenly I realized the pod had placed *me* in the *center* of their pod!!! Whoa! I was totally aware of an immense sense of honor and awe. Dolphins tend to swim with the weakest swimmer of the pod in the center while the stronger ones surround, support, and protect. Every cell of my being resonated, feeling love all around me.

As I was holding my breath, I began to increase my pace, thinking I needed to stay with them. When in fact, they were actually letting me set the pace of the swim. As I sped up, they sped up at exactly the same pace. There was no separation. We were swimming as one. I realized then, I would not be able to hold that pace much longer on one breath, so I slowed down and seamlessly they slowed with me. My lesson, "We are one. We are connected to all of life!" I truly felt the dolphins gifted me with that life-enriching truth by allowing me to swim within their pod. What a blessing!

When I needed to surface to breathe, the pod spiral danced and peeled away from the point I ascended. I immediately took a breath and descended again. I found myself blissfully surrounded by two moms and their babies, spiraling around me as I twirled in elated celebration of this heart-awakening experience! Again, heartfelt gratitude permeated my being! This lesson filled me with joy as I continued to dance my life on land enthusiastically awaiting my next opportunity with my friends in the sea.

Trust

Sometime later, I was presenting two of my dolphin-inspired Nia playshops, "Reclaiming the Heart" and "Water Dance," in Charleston, S.C. (Let me explain: Nia technique eloquently blends energies of Eastern and Western art forms to invite balance for our whole being: body, mind, spirit, and emotion. The teaching and tools of Nia embrace self-acceptance and personal responsibility as well as all the lessons so lovingly demonstrated by the dolphins. While vacationing in Kauai, I discovered *Nai'a* in Hawaiian means dolphin. No mistake there!)

My hostess, Stephaney Robison, had told me about a recent encounter she had with a dolphin while walking the beach by her home early one morning. She was sounding and singing from her heart when a friendly dolphin surfaced to acknowledge her greeting.

I had a lot on my mind, so the next morning I followed her footsteps and went for a walk along the same beach. I began singing and sounding, hoping to draw the dolphins in to play. Suddenly, I realized that I was singing softly to myself, much like I was keeping my thoughts and feelings to myself.

I stopped at the edge of the shoreline, faced the water and heard a loud and clear message inside my heart: "Trust. Let your voice be heard." I could feel their presence and knew this lesson was delivered from the dolphins.

In that moment, my voice released with powerful intention and complete trust, singing in celebration. Simultaneously, as I released my voice I saw, just 10 feet in front of me, a solo dolphin surface, connecting with me eye to eye. As long as I continued to sing, the dolphin gracefully swam parallel to the shoreline. When I saw people walking toward me, I hesitated to sound, at which point the dolphin disappeared from my sight.

This particular life lesson is one that I continue to be tested on. I have often withheld "speaking my truth," lacking a conviction to honestly take care of my own needs, thoughts, and feelings. I thank the dolphins for reminding me of the abundant joy I receive when I trust and use my voice openly, honestly, and confidently.

Just BE

During a glorious 10-day vacation in Kauai, my husband and I chose to join Joan Ocean on a wild dolphin swim off the shore of Hawaii, known as the Big Island. Meeting Joan on the morning of our swim, we felt the energy very similar to my previous experiences playing with wild dolphins. Her eyes sparkled and her peaceful, graceful presence warmed my heart. We were honored to join in on the first of a 4-day workshop she co-facilitated.

Before we boarded the boat, our group gathered in a circle on the dock. Each participant was introduced warmly. Joan led us in a guided meditation to open our heart centers and invite the dolphins to trust and honor us with their presence. She has been blessed by countless swims with the Hawaiian dolphins. I experienced a radiating energy coursing through my body as she spoke. She was clearly creating space for the dolphins to join us, to trust us, to teach us, to play with us. My heart felt expanded and eager to receive whatever gifts from the sea awaited me on that day.

As we pulled away from the dock, dolphins immediately began to swim toward our boat. Every cell of my being danced with elation. We attempted to swim with them right away. However, they were not ready for us to join them yet and disappeared. Our boat traveled along the coast hoping to find them. We surrendered to the possibility that we may not see them again, so we anchored the boat and snorkeled. As I began to let go of the "outcome" and enjoy our snorkeling on the reef, I heard a shout from the boat, "Dolphins!"

We got back aboard in order to move the boat toward them, inviting them to play in our wake. Soon, dolphins were splashing, dancing, and playing all around us — spinners, spotted, bottlenose. I had never before witnessed such an amazing, entertaining, and heart-expanding sight! Watching their magical dance from the boat was an experience I will always remember. Witnessing the individual pods swimming and rhythmically breathing as one and synergistically dancing with all the other pods created for me a magnificent image of our interwoven web of life. I felt connected to their breath, their dance, completely and totally present and *alive!*

We quickly, and as gently as humans can, entered the water to swim with our friends. I excitedly dove under to receive a harmonious choral performance like none I've ever heard before. Their song resonated through me. I felt their sonar waves healing my soul. I have no idea how many dolphins were present, yet I know I felt an immense and radiant joy.

I had asked the dolphins many times during the swim what their lesson was for me now. Nothing came. Perhaps "nothing" was my answer. What greater truth could I possibly witness through sight, sound, feeling, and *be-ing* completely present — a perfect gift from a full chorus of teachers. "JUST BE" permeates my heart from this amazing excursion. I know I will return to learn more from Joan and our friends in the sea. And as they say "thank you" in Hawaiian, *mahalo*.

Reflecting back to the poster I have in my office, "To live on the land, we must learn from the sea," this message resonates great truth for me in my life journey. The lessons I've learned from the stray man-of-war tentacle, the dolphin encounters, and numerous other life-enriching experiences with marine life — from the smallest marine life forms to swimming for a breathtaking timeless moment beside a 17-foot whale shark — all have greatly enriched my life.

My heart tells me that the universal truths I learned from the sea are reflected in nature all around us. These lessons have given me an opportunity to continue walking my journey of awakening and feeling at home on land in the same way I so passionately identify with the water environment.

The messages in the dolphin stories reside in my heart. I recall them whenever I get stuck and fall into past patterns of limitation and fear. They are foundation seeds for my teaching as well as principles for all my relationships with others and with myself.

I believe we all feel each other's pain and joy. I believe that we are all dancing in an astounding interwoven web on this planet. My hope, by sharing my journey, is that my stories touch your heart in some way. Take what your heart connects with and "with a breath of kindness, blow the rest away."

The life lessons I learned from dolphins and my friends in the sea —

- Just breathe.
- Lighten up. Play more.
- Trust the process of life unfolding.
- Create the space for your intention.
- Surrender expectations and the need to control outcomes.
- Accept the gifts of each moment. Accept your choices.
- We are one. We are connected to all life.
- Trust. Let your voice be heard.
- Just BE. Embrace the moment with complete and total presence.

Enjoy your dance on the planet, my friend. May our hearts cross paths as we journey forward with dolphin joy!

Knowing Who We Are and
Where We Come From Frees Us All

Sylva Dvorak, MS, CHES

In 1996, Sylva Dvorak had an idea — a plan to develop a strategic global marketing and communications firm whose philosophy emphasized a spirit of compassion for each other and the world in which we live. Taking her years of experience in consulting, developing, implementing, and evaluating health programs, she founded Atman International, a successful strategic marketing and communications company with expertise in health management, behavior change, professional education and training, and social marketing.

Born in the Czech Republic, Sylva attended the University of Michigan where she earned both her bachelor's and master's degrees. She is also a Certified Health Education Specialist (CHES). It was at the University of Michigan that she developed an interest in bettering people's lives through improved health, not only for those in the United States, but abroad as well.

Atman's projects since 1996 have reflected this desire, from educational interventions and health promotion for a community in Brazil to the development of a lifestyle improvement program that has been translated into 26 languages for use worldwide in the creation of patient health management programs for cardiovascular disease. It has been implemented in seven countries.

In her role at Atman, Sylva has served as a consultant on international projects for companies such as Bristol Myers Squibb and Amway Corporation/Nutrilite. Sylva has made numerous presentations and written and conducted training programs for employer groups/employees, health professionals and for various clients.

More recently, Sylva is also consulting with companies in the emerging conscious business development movement. Sylva's ethics support a belief in the global interrelatedness of life, business, and government. This belief is part of her personal awareness and forms the foundation of all her work.

Sylva Dvorak
President
Atman International
15332 Antioch St. #406
Pacific Palisades, CA 90272
(310) 390-0428
(310) 398-3297 fax
sylva@atmanint.com

My Story

The details about how I came to the United States have been buried in my heart and psyche for over 30 years. Those of us who are refugees follow an unspoken oath of silence never to discuss the past or the pains associated with our common experiences of escape to freedom and abandonment of our beloved lands, families, histories, possessions, identities, responsibilities, and pride. It has been our understanding that we are just supposed to be grateful for everything we have, and the only way of proving this is to appear to deny anything that has gone before. Could it be that if we acknowledge our own histories that we would be sent away by the country we claim as our new home, once again losing everything?

Let me start from the beginning. I was born in a little mountain town of Celadna in what was formerly Czechoslovakia and is now the Czech Republic. I can remember the joy I felt at the times I would visit my grandparents' home. In the mornings, I would walk with my grandfather to the local bakery. My grandmother would yell after us, "Don't let *deda* (grandpa in Czech) buy the salted rolls." She said that too much salt was not good for our health. Upon our return from the bakery, my grandma who was blind, would inspect the rolls to feel if there were salt crystals on top. Of course, she would find our favorite salted ones and scold us. The incredible taste and smell of those warm rolls with butter will always be embedded in my mind.

Other vivid memories are not so sweet (or salty!). Military tanks rolled down the street as I walked with my father. He held my hand tightly. He did not say anything and I never asked why they were there, but I felt the tension in the air by how hard my father squeezed my hand.

It was the time of Prague Spring. Soviet Union troops had invaded Czechoslovakia.

My very last memory of my native land was being told by my parents that we were going on a family holiday to Yugoslavia where I would see the ocean. In July 1969 my family, with the help of my grandfather who had been an underground spy in World War II, escaped into Austria. My father was part of the resistance movement against the Soviet invasion. Because of his involvement, there had been "threats" placed on the family. Thus my parents decided it would be best to flee our beloved homeland.

We were all anxious the day we made the crossing. My sister and I didn't know why we felt that way. We thought it was for the excitement of our upcoming holiday. Little did we know it would be the last time we would see any of our relatives, except for my grandparents, for the next 20 years. (My family could not communicate openly with all my other relatives who remained in Czechoslovakia until after the Velvet Revolution of 1989.)

I remember clutching my teddy bear Misha and having to hand him over to the armed guards for inspection. We were placed into several refugee camps. At their best, such camps are terrible. We were fortunate, we made it out before the borders completely shut down. Five months later, I did finally see the ocean, but it was from an airplane as we flew to the United States.

My parents, my sister, and I arrived in the United States in December, 1969 with two small suitcases and my teddy bear. My parents had left everything they had worked for in exchange for the promise of freedom and future opportunities for my sister and myself.

Sylva Dvorak

One of my first experiences when we arrived in New York was my parents pointing to the "American robust, red-clothed Santa Claus" who looked so different than our thin, tall and white-clothed St. Nicholas. This Santa scared me. When they tried to get me to pose with Santa so that they could take a picture of me sitting on Santa's lap, I refused. Through my childhood, I never did sit on Santa's lap.

My early days in school in this country were challenging. I did not speak the language and looked and acted differently than other children. At a young age the last thing you want to be is different. The other children often teased me because of these differences. But through the pain of these early experiences, I learned to value my heritage and gained a curiosity about other cultures. It gave me a tremendous will to survive, to appreciate everything that I have, to value freedom, and always to vote because I have the privilege.

Perhaps it is this "difference" that gave me the curiosity later in my life to travel and experience and study other cultures. Perhaps it was also a "seeking" for the familiar or a place of belonging that fascinated me about distant lands and their customs and rituals.

In Czechoslovakia when I was a baby, my grandmother had to smuggle me into a church to be baptized. From the age of 5, I started seeking spiritual truths and from then on embarked on a lifetime spiritual journey within. My early experiences also gave me the drive to succeed and have my own business because, in this free land, that was possible. As a refugee whose family had sacrificed everything for me to have this opportunity, it was my obligation.

For the most part, I believe that from being a refugee I gained a deep compassion for others from other cultures and those struggling to fit in.

I have had a lifetime commitment to humanitarian work. I think it started out in order to ease some of my guilt for the rest of my relatives who had been left behind in Czechoslovakia and for those who had been persecuted for my family's freedom. That's what put me on the path to work in the area of health care and to try to help others from getting sick. In my unconscious mind, if I contributed and healed others, I eased the burden of my guilt. The guilt of the survivor, the one who has been chosen to live and carry life for those who were left behind, but who never made the choice herself. Although I no longer take on this responsibility, I have a passion for understanding cultures, in healing rituals, and how they can be used in contemporary health care.

I started my marketing and communications company Atman International in 1996. I chose *atman,* a Sanskrit word, for my company name because it symbolizes unity — the global interrelatedness of life, business, and government. Understanding ourselves and our world in regard to culture is one aspect of this interrelatedness.

Atman International approaches each project and challenge with an understanding that any solution presented affects individuals, families, companies, and the community. Therefore, all must be part of the solution. We try to integrate culture and cultural consciousness, competence, and sensitivity into all of our projects, especially projects related to health care. These projects have included health management programs in countries such as Australia and Spain to social marketing campaigns promoting condom use in Brazil to the creation of numerous education and training programs. More recently, we are consulting on conscious business development for companies either starting up or companies looking to differentiate themselves in the marketplace.

The message is simple and straightforward: If we understand the impact of where we are from and open ourselves to accepting others because of their own cultural experiences, we gain tremendous compassion for others and "exchange" a healing experience with them.

I am an American businesswoman. I am Czech. I am proud and happy to be all that I am. And I am committed to my career and life's work involving the integration of my life's experience into my profession in order to contribute to the growth and benefit of all people of all cultures in the spirit of Atman — unity.

Knowing Who We Are and Where We Come From Frees Us All

What is cultural consciousness, compassion, and sensitivity? To truly understand this, we first need to look at ourselves, who we are, where we come from, and the impact of our own culture on our lives. This introspection and understanding will "free" us to be able to objectively look at another culture with an open mind and heart. Understanding the role of culture in our own lives will give us a framework from which to look at differences among other cultures in terms of how individuals think and behave, which is crucial to our own health and the health of our world.

To understand your own cultural identity ask yourself these questions:

- When and what is your earliest recollection of your cultural identity?

- What were the positive and negative experiences of your cultural identity while growing up?

- What thoughts, feelings, or actions by others are the most offensive to you from that cultural base?

- What negative thoughts, feelings, or actions have you experienced in the past about other cultures?

- What are the positive and negative influences that your cultural identity has had on your career?

- What do you feel is the most valuable or important attribute of your cultural identification?

Cultural competence is a huge topic, so here we'll focus on just a few examples in the health care industry to help you begin the process of looking at these differences in your own workplace or community and apply the process in your own context.

Understanding the significance of culture is very important because, in the general community, intolerance toward diversity invites tension and hostility among different ethnic groups. In the business world, not paying attention to cultural differences can mean the difference between success and failure of a business transaction. In health care settings, ignoring cultural factors may be hazardous to a person's health.

To be culturally conscious or competent is to realize and accept that our own culture's way of doing things is not necessarily the universal or superior way. Keep an open mind and stay flexible and respect things we do not understand — yet accept them as being valid.

We all need to be conscious of certain cultural differences. Let us examine a vast amount of information about our world and its cultures and take a first step toward integrating this information:

Stereotyping: When you assume that people of the same racial or ethnic category believe, value, and behave the same way, you are stereotyping. Be aware of the dangers of such beliefs if you want to understand other cultures. We tend to categorize others because such generalization can help us in communicating with people when we first meet them. Generalization helps us to deal with unfamiliar situations, but when we fall into the trap of stereotyping, such generalization may close us off to new experiences.

Nobody wants to be stereotyped. Everyone is unique in his or her own way, skills, characteristics, and abilities. By accepting the diversity of people, you can learn from others. Understanding general cultural trends helps to make you more sensitive to people of other cultures.

- Keep in mind that nobody likes to be stereotyped based on outward appearances. Everyone is unique in his or her own way, skills, characteristics, and abilities.

- See people as individuals first, without making cultural assumptions.

Categorizing: Beware of categorizing. Although people are categorized into broad groups such as Asian, African American, or Hispanic, there are a multitude of distinct cultures within each category. For example: Asian typically refers to people from countries such as Philippines, Cambodia, Thailand, Indonesia, Japan, China, and Korea. Someone of Thai descent sees himself as very culturally different from someone of Japanese descent.

To be truly culturally aware is to realize that many factors such as these influence the impact of a person's culture on his or her life:

- Social support system
- Values

- Communication styles

- Views of health and illness

- Time orientation

- Space orientation

- Decision making

- Health practices

- Genetic differences

- Rituals

Social support systems are organizations, groups, or institutions that help establish a cultural identity. They can be used as vehicles to meet a particular need and play an important role in shaping values, beliefs, and attitudes. The church is one example of a social support system that can meet not only a spiritual need but the physical, educational, and social needs of its members and their families. Understanding and accepting cultural social support systems is essential in bridging the gap between the organization and the individual or community you are trying to reach. An African proverb says "it takes an entire village to raise a child."

When it comes to **values**, let's talk a little bit about Americanism. The majority of the United States is composed of Caucasian, or White, Americans. Historically, White Americans come from many European countries. In early American history, waves of immigrants were thought to become part of a melting pot that created a single all-American culture. However, this melting pot model may not necessarily be the truth. Researchers are finding that each ethnic and minority group has retained some of its own traditional values, while adopting the values of the broader American society. The so-called typical American values can be quite different from values in other cultures. Yet, in actuality, there is *no* such thing as typical American! Americans come in all colors, shapes, and sizes, and from many different cultures.

Be aware of these factors to raise your cultural consciousness:

- **Decision-making** is an important part of the American medical care system. Usually we believe individuals have decision-making power. But this is not the case in what is considered "old" cultures. Acceptable health practices vary among cultures and are often determined by the culture's decision-making structure. The types of health care sought by individuals in some cultures are often not a result of their own decision.

- **Time orientation** refers to whether people see time in terms of the past, present, or future. Most cultures tend to emphasize one over the other. In general, in countries with economies based on agriculture, people tend to be more relaxed about time. The pace is slower and more attuned to nature's rhythms. Whereas, many people in industrialized nations pay attention to clock time. In big cities (even in developing nations), usually people are required to keep schedules.

- In many cultures there is no separation between **religious beliefs and medical treatment.** Truly, even in American culture, the critically ill patient frequently prays to God. This is the position of the health versus medical practitioner. To work with people most effectively is where body, mind, and spirit come together.

- **Communication styles** vary among cultures. Having at least a broad understanding of different communication styles will help you communicate more effectively. Styles of communication include both verbal and nonverbal. The meaning of specific verbal and nonverbal signals can be distinctly different between cultures. For example:

Oral vs. written. Spoken communication is considered to be more personal and is the predominant and traditional means of information transmission among African American, Asian/Pacific, American Indian/Alaskan, and Latino communities.

Verbal communication. Calling a person by his or her first name should never be done especially when first meeting someone or if the person is older or distinguished by professional rank unless given specific permission by the individual. In our multicultural world this is often offensive. But you will not be told it is so because that is not acceptable with the person being offended either. So how do you do it? Ask! Ask the individual first how they would like to be addressed.

Nonverbal communication. The meaning of body language and gestures varies from culture to culture. There are numerous examples of nonverbal communication. Here are just a few:

Direct or indirect style. Americans tend to communicate with a direct style, while Latino/Hispanic, Pacific Islander, and Asian cultures use more indirect, subtle styles in order to avoid conflict and create a smooth interaction. *Example: Americans usually don't hesitate in asking personal questions, and seeing a therapist or support groups are completely acceptable. This is not so with many other cultures. Privacy is respected and personal things are kept within the family.*

Eye contact. In some Latin, U.S. Southern Black, Asian and Pacific Islander, and American Indian communities, direct eye contact is considered rude and disrespectful, especially,y when talking with an older person or authority figure. However, Americans tend to see a lack of eye contact as deception, rudeness, and defiance. *Example: In Mexico, when talking with an older person or authority figure, downcast eyes may denote respect and attention.*

- **Rituals** are ancient and archetypal ceremonies. Ceremonies have been used throughout parts of the world since the beginning of time. They have significant cultural meaning in helping individuals go through life transitions and for mental, emotional, and physical healing. In America, outside of the Native American culture, such ceremonies are not a traditional part of the culture.

These are just a few examples of ways to increase our cultural consciousness. Any meaningful discussion of cultural awareness and its application in life requires introspective examination of ourselves and how we live and relate to others. It is a commitment to a way of being and living that is at the very least a process of transformation for the individual concerned and an act of commitment to life that incrementally improves and touches everything we come in contact with each day.

Our motivations toward this decision and the actions that follow can be personal, community-related, professional or financial, but they require the same process. The very process itself opens us to learning experiences at every level that inexorably and irrevocably change us, enriching each of us, our families, and the communities and business environments that we create.

A quote by Toni Morrison sums it up the best. She wrote that "the function of freedom is to free someone else."

Life/Work Balance from the Inside Out

Deborah Kern, PhD

Deborah Kern, PhD, helps people experience the body-mind connection — that is, the link between the body and emotions or life issues.

It's a path she's explored personally and professionally over the past 20 years. Coming from a traditional health science background, to awakening both personally and professionally to holistic ways of thinking and exploring healing, she is an ardent proponent of body wisdom. She shares this power with other health professionals and the public in her entertaining keynotes.

Her journey has included nursing studies, heading the weight management division of a hospital, studying herbal medicine with the indigenous women of Costa Rica, and earning her PhD in health sciences. Not content to just read and study about the topic, Dr. Kern has been an active practitioner, working as a personal trainer, fitness instructor, competitive race walker, yoga practitioner, and spa director. Today her passions include writing and speaking, as well as running her own wellness consulting practice in Alabama.

Dr. Kern is the author of *Everyday Wellness for Women,* the first of a series of books that encapsulates a proactive approach to health and well-being. Helping people make positive lifestyle changes is a way of life for Deborah — starting with herself! She's the 40-something wife and mom of a toddler and a teen and combines family responsibilities with a demanding career, just like the people she counsels.

She helps people "feel" the science of the body-mind connection. Through their active participation, people can actually see the patterns in their lives that disconnect body and mind. Deborah gives them tools to reconnect and use this power to enhance not only their physical health but their work, their relationships, and their spiritual well-being.

As she says, "My passion is to help people learn from the wisdom of their bodies and help them make peace between the intellect and the heart."

Deborah Kern, PhD
605 County Road 1184
Cullman, AL 35057
(256) 775-3716
www.deborahkern.com
dr.deb@deborahkern.com

My Story

Looking from the outside in, my life was perfect — and I had worked hard to create it. At the age of 30, I had all the worldly accoutrements of success. With an MBA, my career had advanced from nursing and health education to a management position in a hospital. I was married to a successful businessman, lived in a beautiful home, was a member of the Junior League, regularly attended church, taught aerobic dance after work, competed in 10k races, ate healthy food, maintained low body fat and high aerobic capacity, and was almost always "peppy."

Then, within three months, I lost my marriage, my pregnancy, and, because I was so shocked and depressed, my job. Everything I had created and dreamed about had vanished. I felt as if the carpet had been ripped out from under my feet. But it was precisely this traumatic time of my life that ripped away all the false notions I held true and provided me a new understanding of life.

I had spent the first 30 years of my life trying to do the "right" thing without ever knowing who I was, what my purpose for being here was, or what I truly wanted out of life. I regard this difficult time as a huge blessing because it forced me to find my authentic self and re-create an authentic life.

Did my life fall into place overnight? Of course not! Will the path I took be the same as yours? Probably not. But I hope that sharing my journey will help awaken your inner knowing and give you courage to follow your heart.

I remember driving along the beltway in Washington, D.C., during this tough time of my life. How easy it would have been to simply swerve off a bridge and end all the agony. Then it dawned on me that people died every day in car accidents on this 12-lane highway, and that if God had kept me safe this far, there must be a reason for my being here.

In a split second I made a major mental shift. Instead of wanting to end my life, I decided I was alive "on purpose" and that I must be here for a purpose. So I decided to stay here and figure out what my purpose was.

Many earth angels helped me through this life transition. One of them was a nurse I worked with at the hospital. She allowed me to live in her guest room while I pieced myself back together. In her loving embrace I had the luxury of time. I didn't have to hurry and make any rash decisions about where I would live or what I would do. Within a few months, I felt compelled to return to my hometown of Dallas, Texas, and enroll in a doctoral program. I wanted to stay in the health profession and have a role as a teacher.

In the beginning, I followed the usual course of studies. During my second semester, however, something happened. I attended a workshop at a fitness convention in which the Nia technique was presented (pronounced *KNEE-uh*).

Nia is a holistic cardiovascular movement form, which was created by Debbie and Carlos Rosas. As Debbie and Carlos led us through simple movements, I experienced very strong emotions that left me drenched not only in sweat but also in tears. This was my first experience in connecting how the mind, body, and emotions relate.

I was so moved by the experience that I decided to take their teacher training course — and the whole course of my studies changed. From that point forward I sought ways to incorporate holistic modalities into my coursework. I learned Healing Touch, studied Native American Shamanism, attended Pleasure Principle workshops led by Karen Carrier, studied and apprenticed Ayurvedic medicine, lived and studied yoga at the Integral Yoga Institute, and studied herbal medicine from a group of women in Costa Rica.

Not only did I learn a whole new way of being a health professional but also my personal life began to heal. Our professional lives and personal lives cannot be separated. Whatever happens in our professional lives impacts our personal lives and vice versa.

In retrospect I can see that had I not been so wounded I would not have been as open to learning these "alternative" healing methods. When I was under the illusion that my life was perfect, I had no motivation to do the hard work of listening to my body, expressing my emotions, or heeding the call of my spirit. In this way, the stumbling block was indeed an exquisite stepping-stone.

Now, 13 years later, I am grateful for the gifts I received during that difficult transition and have been less afraid of the transitions I have faced: remarrying, becoming a step mom, giving birth to my first baby at age 40, having total urinary incontinence for the following three years, experiencing severe postpartum depression coupled with midlife hormonal changes, going through my husband's business difficulties, juggling a demanding travel schedule with mothering, being transferred from a large metroplex in Texas to a rural town in Alabama.

Sometimes I have felt incredibly overwhelmed, but I always remember the experience I had while driving on the Washington, D.C. beltway and remind myself that it is no accident that I'm here. Once I remember that I am here for a purpose, I begin the healing process again…and again and again.

Life/work balance is a barometer for well-being: personal, family, and community well-being. This chapter is not a prescription for how you should live your life. It is simply a compilation of some of the tools I have used to continually address the issue of life/work balance in my own life. May you find some blessing by reading it.

Life/Work Balance from the Inside Out

Simplify Your Life

Finding a way to live the simple life is one of life's supreme complications.

T. S. Eliot

Whenever I feel that my life and work are out of balance, I take a look at what I can simplify. I believe this step is necessary for all of us. The sheer complexity of our lives causes internal distress and can wreak havoc on our bodies. Our hearts get overstimulated, our immune systems become suppressed, hormones get out of balance, and our reproductive systems no longer function properly. But because we are addicted to complexity, we can't find a way out. I know. I've been there, and I've spent the past 10 years consciously finding ways to simplify my life. In the third year of "life simplification," I became acutely aware of the positive impact this plan was having on my health and on my ability to manage life/work balance.

Poverty is involuntary and debilitating, whereas simplicity is voluntary and enabling.

Duane Elgin

How much do we need?

Sometimes life simplification requires a paradigm shift. Have you ever seen the house where your parents grew up and asked, "How did you survive with that tiny bathroom? Where are the closets? How could five kids share two bedrooms?" What your parents called luxuries, you're calling necessities: walk-in closets, master bathroom suites, separate bedrooms, a phone in every room, cellular phones, home computers, TVs, and VCRs. Not to mention espresso machines, bread makers, faxes, and satellite television.

One reason for our inability to achieve simplicity is that we clutter our lives with far more than we actually need. As Will Rogers once said, "We buy these things we don't need, with money we don't have, to impress people we don't even like!" Much of our leisure time is spent taking care of or paying for things we really didn't need in the first place. The problem is we've been doing it so long, we don't realize that something is amiss.

One of the best ways to "break the spell" of over-consumption and over-complexity is to visit less-developed countries. In 1994 I spent a month in the rain forest of Costa Rica to learn local herbal medicine from a group of women. I stayed in a two-room hut with a family of seven and shared a double bed (the only bed) with two teen-aged girls.

One afternoon, as I was weeding the herb garden, the younger girl stepped off the school bus and came running over to ask me a question. "Is it true," she asked, "that people in your country eat pineapple out of a can?"

"Yes," I said.

"Well, I never want to go there!" she responded. And if you've ever tasted freshly harvested pineapple, you'll understand why.

On another occasion, as we lay in bed before falling asleep, the older girl asked, "Is it true that the women in your country have to work so hard that they give their children to strangers to take care of during the day?"

I didn't know how to respond. First of all, the women in my country don't work any harder than the women of this village — who begin work at 5 in the morning and engage in hard physical labor outdoors until the sun sets, and then work indoors until 9 or 10 at night.

I realized that I was feeling sorry for these girls for not having the opportunities I have had while they were feeling sorry for me! Now, as a working mom, I am reminded of these questions often and constantly re-engineer my work to be able to spend quality time with my children and husband. And when I grab a quick lunch at the airport, I am reminded of the fresh pineapple, papaya, bananas, and mango of the rain forest and wonder what I can do to bring those "simple" pleasures into my busy, modern life.

Action Step: Life simplification is a personal choice and an ongoing process. To begin, examine all areas of your life and determine five areas that can be simplified. Then do them!

Examples:

- Let your bed go unmade or your kids go without a bath every now and then.
- Drop membership on a committee.
- Eat simpler foods.

- Plant ground cover that requires little maintenance.
- Keep things longer (cars, clothes, home décor, for example).
- Clear out the clutter.
- Don't watch TV.

Breathe!

Whenever my life and work are out of balance, I notice I can barely take a deep breath. (Please note that the only way you will notice this is if you pay attention. I have learned how to be aware of my body through Nia and yoga.) We have a hard time breathing when we are stressed for a number of reasons. One reason is that holding the breath is the best way to suppress emotions. Whenever your life is out of balance, you will certainly have many emotions. Have you ever noticed that when you are trying not to laugh aloud in church or trying not to cry in front of a co-worker, you hold your breath?

Another reason we have a hard time breathing is that shallow chest breathing is a physical response to stress. Add to that the cultural imperative for women to have a flat abdomen, and you have the perfect recipe for creating a society of shallow "chest breathers," rather than healthy "abdominal breathers."

Try this exercise:

1. Sit comfortably with your spine elongated.

2. Place one hand on your abdomen below your navel and the other hand on your chest.

3. Now take in a full, deep breath and pay attention to which hand moves first — chest hand or belly hand.

If the hand on your chest moved first, you are breathing like the majority of women in our society. This breath is performed by expanding and lifting the rib cage, which only fills the upper and middle portions of the lungs. This is about 1/7 of your lung's capacity — not much. Chest breathing is also called "stress" breathing.

If the hand on your abdomen moved first, you are using the diaphragm to help bring air into the lower lobes of the lungs. This is so important because there is more blood available for oxygen exchange in the lower parts of the lungs. To completely expel the breath from the lower lobes, the abdominal muscles have to engage to squeeze out the residual air (which makes breathing a wonderful abdominal muscle toning activity when done correctly).

For a deeply relaxing breath, the goal is to breathe so that the abdomen expands first and, as the air rises, the chest fills and then the collarbones rise. When we breathe like this, we get superb oxygen exchange, our hearts don't have to work overtime, our blood pressure tends to lower, and we are able to experience and express our emotions.

Action Step: Choose a way to remind yourself to breathe deeply during the day.
Examples:

- Set your watch to beep every hour. Each hour take three deep breaths.
- Every time the train, car, or subway makes a stop, take three deep breaths.
- While waiting for someone to answer the phone, take deep breaths.
- Add positive affirmations to your breathing such as one suggested by Thich Nhat Hanh: "Breathing in I calm my body. Breathing out I smile."

Calm Your Mind

Meditation is not an evasion, it is a serene encounter with reality.

Thich Nhat Hanh

Meditation is the calming of the mind so we can listen to God instead of the babbling that goes on in our heads all day.

Sister Mary McGehee

I believe it is important to simplify your life — and once you begin a meditation practice, it will become even clearer to you. If you are like most women, your mind operates much like a computer system. You have multiple applications operating at the same time, and with a click of the mouse you can switch from one application to another. That's why you are able to give a marketing presentation, while suddenly remembering that you need to buy your best friend a birthday gift and plan what you are going to wear for dinner that night. Or you can make dinner while talking on the phone, watch the baby, and call out spelling words for your 10-year-old — and never miss a beat! Unfortunately, this gift of multi-tasking can become a curse when we can't figure out how to stop the chaos in our minds and calm down.

There are many methods of meditation. Although the benefits of Transcendental Meditation are the best documented, tests at the Thorndike Memorial Laboratory of Harvard show that a similar technique used with any sound, phrase, prayer, or mantra brings forth the same physiologic changes noted during Transcendental Meditation: decreased oxygen consumption, decreased carbon-dioxide elimination, and decreased rate of breathing.

Meditation begins with concentration — focusing your mind on any one point. It is important to note that there are many ways to meditate, and many choices for focal points. I often say to my beginning students that there are as many ways to meditate as there are people. You can learn meditation methods from books, tapes, or classes. Just do it!

Action Step: Choose a way to calm and focus your mind and commit to practicing this at least once a day for at least five minutes.

Examples:

- Focus on a word, phrase, or image. Whenever your mind wanders, return your mind to your chosen focus.

- Use commute time on a bus, train, or subway to practice your meditation.

- Use time spent doing routine chores to focus your mind on the present moment.

- Before you get out of bed, sit up and spend five minutes in meditation.

- Before going to sleep, spend five minutes breathing deeply, relaxing your body and releasing thoughts from the day.

Deborah Kern

Know Your Purpose

To help me keep my life and work in balance, I continually ask myself if what I am doing is in alignment with my purpose. From a Steven Covey lecture I attended in 1992, I still have the outline from A. Roger Merrill's book *Connections: Quadrant II Time Management* on how to create a mission statement. In the past I have used this as a map for creating a mission statement. Here's the process:

1. Identify a few people who have been very influential in your life. Then list the qualities you most admire in these people.

2. Define what you want to be, to do, and to have.

3. Define your life roles (such as mother, manager, sister, daughter, lover, friend and so on). Then write a brief statement of how you would most like to be described in that particular role.

4. Having clearly identified the previous items, draft a mission statement.

5. Regularly update your mission statement.

For many years I used this process as a way to help me remember my purpose and a way for me to judge whether something (like a relationship, a job, or a purchase) was in alignment with my purpose or not.

Although this is a great way to determine your mission, I now prefer a body-centered approach to knowing my mission and whether or not I am in alignment with my purpose. I use a process called Phoenix Rising Yoga Therapy to do this. In it, a practitioner (or in my case, I can do it for myself) holds you in certain yoga positions and facilitates a conversation between you and your body. This process cuts out endless loops of analytical thought, questioning, and self-doubt. It allows your true self to speak to you. Because it is a complex process, I recommend that you find a Phoenix Rising Yoga practitioner in your area and receive a session.

Action Step: Using either the analytical approach or the body-centered approach, ask yourself the questions: "What is my purpose on earth?" "What are my talents and gifts?" Then ask yourself if all areas of your life are in line with your purpose and whether you are using your gifts and talents.

A Daily Practice

In a culture where workaholics are admired, it is very easy for your life and work to get out of balance. That is why I make it a daily practice to breathe deeply, calm my mind, simplify what I can, and then check in with myself to see if how I am living aligns with my purpose for being here. Even with these practices, I still find myself out of balance — but I don't stay that way as long or go as far away from center as I used to before I had these practices. I hope they help you as much as they have helped me!

Resources:

The Nia Technique: (800) 762-5762 or www.nia-nia.com
Phoenix Rising Yoga Therapy: (800) 288-9642 or www.pryt.com
Everyday Wellness for Women by Deborah Kern. To order:
(256) 775-3716 or www.deborahkern.com

One Woman's Journey

Elaine Sullivan

My name is Elaine Marie Albracht Sullivan. I was born in Nazareth, a small rural community in the Texas Panhandle where I lived for 14 years with my family — my parents, three sisters, and five brothers. Although we were poor and life was simple, I never lacked in basic needs. My childhood was spent creating imaginative ways to play, working on the farm, visiting relatives, and worshipping in the Catholic Church, which was the center of this little town's life.

And so begins the life story of a woman who has helped so many others write their stories. Elaine goes on…

At age 15 I joined the Benedictine Convent in Fort Smith, Ark. At age 16 I was a novice wearing a religious habit. Vocation, as Fredrick Buechner asserts, is "the place where your deep gladness meets the world's deep needs." My calling would lead me on a journey that took many paths as I listened to the small still voice within. At age 18 I began my teaching career in an African-American parish where the harsh reality of prejudice and hatred entered my sheltered life. As a result I became a strong advocate for civil rights and social justice.

During the years I taught school, I pursued my degree in the summer vacation periods. After almost 15 years I completed my graduate work having had experience as a teacher in all 12 grades, a principal of two schools, a full-time graduate student, and an active member of a Benedictine Community.

In 1968 I took a leave from my religious community and began working as a counselor and instructor of psychology at the University of Wisconsin, Stevens Point. There I met my husband, Joe Sullivan, who resigned the active priesthood. We were married in 1972, almost 30 years ago. Our two sons, Kevin, 27, and Kieran, 25, are the joy of our lives today.

In 1972 we moved to Chicago where I began my work at Oakton Community College as a counselor and a professor of psychology. This would be the place I launched the work that has become my lifework. In 1972 my dean called me into his office and asked me to do something to serve the women 25 years of age and older who were beginning to trickle into our college as returning college students. He said, "We have no staff and no money." I jokingly said, "I used to walk on water, but I don't anymore."

I faced this challenge by searching to find a way to meet the needs of women older than 25. I was 36 and had written my auto-biography for completion of my graduate work the previous year. Putting my story in writing had been one of the most significant experiences in my life. Because I gained so much understanding of my own inner journey, I designed a course for 15 returning-to-college women who would spend 16 weeks writing and sharing their own personal stories.

In 1972, I could find very little published on journaling or writing an autobiography; however, I believed I could make it happen. The dean supported the idea of designating a section of Applied Psychology for women 25-years-old and older. That spring, I offered the first course. When it filled immediately, I opened a second section. Four semesters later the college was offering 12 sections of this course. I was hiring and training teachers to work with the power of stories. We were building a community of women who had written and shared their stories.

Deep in my heart I wish I could have captured on paper the excitement of those first years. I had stumbled on an incredible process and slowly began to realize the breadth and depth of this autobiographical writing and the power of shared story. Women were coming to our college connecting with women in circles of shared stories. Together we were discovering what happens when masks are removed and the true Self is revealed.

For almost 30 years I have taught this class. The lives of so many women in search of the Self has taken me to places I never dreamed I would go. When I finished my master's degree, I was invited into a doctoral program. I had been in school for so many years where I found so much of higher education steeped in linear, logical, objective learning, which left something missing for me. As I thought about a doctorate, I listened to my own deep intuition inviting me to search for a deeper way of knowing.

Eventually, I said "No" to a doctoral program and "Yes" to finding teachers and mentors who would challenge my heart and soul as well as my mind — teachers who would challenge me to explore the world inside myself. I made a pledge to myself to look around this country and find people from whom I could choose to learn — people who would invite me to continue discovering my own inner cosmos. These would be teachers who would also mentor and guide me. This quest for the past 30 years has helped me deepen my own story and the stories of my students.

I spent years studying with teachers in Transactional Analysis and became a Clinician in 1977. I studied and worked with John Travis, MD, studying a holistic approach to health and wellness. Virginia Satir was one of my mentors, as was Jean Houston. I studied with Harville Hendrix and became an Advanced Clinician in Imago Relationship Therapy. I have spent the past three years as a student of Parker Palmer's work in formation. As one of the facilitators of his work, I offer retreats and presentations, which deal with the inner landscape of human beings.

As I have grown and deepened in the understanding of my own story, I have learned to create a safe space for other individuals exploring the meaning of their own stories through a myriad of approaches. Because I started story work at the University of Wisconsin, I was later invited to present my work at the National Wellness Conference, which is held there every summer. For over 20 years, I have presented workshops at this conference on the many aspects of autobiography, journaling, and the exploration of our inner landscapes. Presently, I am on the Board of Directors of the National Wellness Institute.

My years of working with stories in a holistic way have taken me across Canada and the U.S. offering workshops and retreats in education, business, and health care. I have facilitated hundreds of retreats for women and have keynoted major conferences. Presently, I am engaged in very exciting work in leadership development in the home, in education, in hospitals, and in businesses. My recent work in relationship-centered care came from my association with the Fetzer Institute in Kalamazoo, Mich. With a grant from them partnering with Parkland Hospital and Richland College, I am now facilitating a two-year project in Dallas with leaders from the community who are engaged in relationship-centered care explorations.

All of this work — the mind-body-spirit movement, the courage to teach and lead from within, and relationship-centered care — stems from the stories carried in the hearts and souls of human beings and the committed willingness to explore the depth of the inner terrain of our lives both in solitude and in community.

Elaine M. Sullivan, MEd, LPC, LMFT
2929 Marsann Lane
Dallas, TX 75234
(972) 243-5333
Elaine@Sullivan-Associates.com

One Woman's Story

In the beautiful poem *Ask Me,* William Stafford writes, "Ask me whether what I have done is my life." From years of reading and studying thousands of life stories, I know clearly that often the life a person leads is not the same as the life that wants to live in them. In each human life there is a life beneath the surface that is often truer and deeper. Our journeys are about reclaiming and celebrating the True Self, the Self that is our hidden wholeness. Nowhere have I learned more intensely the meaning of our hidden wholeness than in working with people to discover the depth of their stories.

Story writing begins with remembering and retelling — gleaning the deeper patterns within our memories. Memories are the most beautiful realities of our souls, touching what is sacred and personal. Our memories give us our uniqueness because no one has our memories. In story work, as we together explore the castle of memories, we revisit experiences of joy, pain, loss, possibility, growth, expansion — often looking through lenses of discernment and discovering nuggets of gold long forgotten or hidden. As we author our stories, we become the authority on our own lives. We rewrite scripts and dramas, see and view them from different perspectives often gaining clear insights into old patterns that bind the soul.

Direct your inner movie

In groups or dyads, we harvest memories. Since our senses are the windows of our souls, we begin with memories from our childhood of sight, sound, touch, taste, smell. When shared in a group, one person's memory evokes another's memory and the cadence of memories flows. We then explore memories related to emotions: anger, fear, joy, grief, loss, excitement, pain, and pleasure.

Descriptions of grandparents, parents, siblings, and family connections always invite us to look at patterns developed years ago that influence our sense of well-being. Together, we explore patterns that evolved around aspects of wellness: physical, emotional, spiritual, social, intellectual, and occupational. What is modeled, what is expressed or not expressed, the early decisions we made and too often kept repressed deep in our unconscious, invite the early development of patterns around these aspects of our lives.

Imagery involving the Inner Child is explored at this time because the Child is the carrier of our stories. Jung said it is the eternal Child that is moving us to wholeness throughout our lives.

Autobiographical work is about making the unconscious more conscious so that we author more of our own story. We keep journals throughout our work to record intuitive insights, to describe forgotten experiences, to see parts of ourselves anew, to wake up to the life that wants to live in us, and to rewrite portions of our stories. We become the directors of our own inner movies.

During story work we explore times of transition in our lives. Perhaps you might recall a natural transition, one caused by loss, death, or change, an ending you may have experienced in one way or another. Transitional times often take you into void times, which invite deep introspection. If you missed these times of reflection, you tend to live your life on the surface without touching the mystery. Reflecting on transitions often challenges you to get past your ego, to face your inner darkness, to rework your deepest beliefs, to rediscover your identity in a new and different way.

The questions, Who am I? What do I value? What are my gifts? What has meaning? often surface. In recalling these transitional times, you may often see and discover aspects of your shadow, the parts of yourself you have denied, could not express, or have repressed. In the shadow you discover gifts and wounds, darkness and light. Revisiting transitional times offers clues for who you have become and who you are becoming. Writing offers you the opportunity to distill those deeper meanings and touch the paradoxes of the soul: shadow and light, wounds and gifts, death and rebirth.

Metaphor opens windows into self

The use of metaphor and deep listening has become central to my work with stories. John Fox, a poet friend of mine, says, "The making of metaphor opens a window where the inner and outer aspects of our lives can join. The metaphoric voice contains the threads that join mind and soul, self and others, self and the natural world, self and God. What once seemed separate is revealed to be made one fabric."

As you begin writing your story, I encourage you to use metaphoric images with questions such as these: "What metaphor might best describe how I, as a child, saw my mother or father?

Now? What metaphor might best describe my first year in school?" Your perceptions, your memories, and their patterns take on new meaning. Metaphors deepen the process of recognition and connection. It stokes the fire of the creative self that was often laid waste by the rigid rules, or the expectations of family and culture.

Playing with metaphor, using imagination, and telling stories opens the heart. It is the opening of the heart I seek in my work with story. Using metaphor to help you deepen your story often invites you to look at the paradoxes of your life: strengths and weaknesses, loneliness and connection, shadows and light, freedom and responsibility. You may begin to question and to learn to live without answers. You may be challenged to stretch your either/or thinking into the realization that paradox is essential in distilling the life of the soul.

Metaphors arise in prose and poetry. Poetry is the language of the soul and consequently invites you, as the storywriter, into your innermost labyrinth. John O'Donohue in his book *Eternal Echoes* says, "When you read a great poem, it reaches deep into the regions of your life and memory and reverberates back to the forgotten or invisible regions of your experience." The song, *The Rose*, has been a theme song for my classes as its metaphors sing of transformation as illustrated by the "seed" as it becomes the "rose."

Creative art is another medium I use in deepening story, in reaching for the story beneath the story. Your story is an art form worked on for a lifetime. Collages, clay, color, and drawings often invite insights as they help release the creative energies within. When you are stuck in uncovering a story, often working with an art form will lead to discoveries never before seen.

Music offers a creative way to listen with your heart. Many forms of music are used to invite reflection and renewal. Music and imagery are woven throughout the writing to open up possibilities. Music is the art form that takes you for a time into another space within your inner castles. Nietzsche says, "A relationship between music and life is not only that of one language to another, it is also the relationship of the perfect world of listening to the whole world of feeling."

I often invite movement to lead a stuck writer. Dance will awaken the soul, which allows new discoveries, new connections to be experienced. Through the years I have learned how our bodies take us into our minds and our minds take us into our bodies. The mind, body, and spirit are one.

Elaine Sullivan

To add another dimension, I use myths, fairy tales, and children's stories to see and understand archetypal patterns of the human psyche, which are found across the centuries. In the great myths there is always a call — some journey lies ahead. To embark on the journey, an ally is called upon so that the pilgrim might have courage in facing dragons, discovering gifts, and returning to community to share their gifts. This is the heroes' journey. This is the heroines' journey. Over and over personal stories become reflective of the larger stories. To uncover the layers of personal journeys, I invite you to study and discuss a book that uses children's stories, *Out of the Skin into the Soul,* authored by my sister and her friend. This book is filled with metaphor and poetic prose. Beautifully written about lifework, it encourages readers to look beneath the facts of their lives to the heart of their experiences.

Celebrating our journey

Story work is heart work. It is seeing with the eyes of our heart and hearing with the ears of our heart. An ancient definition of the heart is the place where the intellect, the emotions, the will, and the spirit converge. Coming from a hierarchal paradigm where the energies of the heart were minimized in favor of linear, rational thought, where the objective world was given much greater credence than the subjective world, where doing was more highly valued than being, and where product was valued over process, we became a culture out of balance. This is the world in which competition was the name of the game not cooperation, where the external world was the reality and the inner world of intuition, emotion, and wisdom was severely minimized, and the art of story telling was lost. In the hierarchical world that devalued the feminine, the power of story to connect and heal was lost. In a world that values the integration of mind, body, and spirit, the polarities of the hierarchical and the partnership ways of viewing and understanding the world are honored, the masculine and feminine energies are balanced.

Relationships are central to stories. As you write and share your stories, connections of the heart are made. Stories help you see more clearly how we are all connected, how we are similar and how we are different and how our uniqueness is a gift to the world. Writers who share their stories build long-lasting relationships. Shared story, whether in education or business, has that power.

When I first started teaching, I was very young and had little training. One evening while I was at the convent, I had a call from a mother who was very frustrated. She said her son was saying his addition facts the way I told him. I asked her what she meant. She said he was saying, "One plus four the son-of-a-bitch is five." I nearly dropped the phone. That was language I did not use in my home. I wondered what kind of family this child had. Then in a flash I remembered what the manual said: Teach them to say, "one plus four, *the sum of which* is five." I laughed so heartily. Later when I started reading stories I realized how many of us still live messages from our cultures, our families, our teachers, our communities that make no sense and tend to rob us of our uniqueness, our authenticity.

Focus on the inner world

Consistent in my work with story is the focus on the inner world. Robert Johnson says, "If we don't do our inner work, it does us." Doing inner work through shared story demands a safe space. To create safe space, no fixing and no advice giving is allowed. In safe space there is no place for judging, criticizing, blaming, or shaming. We learn together to hold each other's stories in wonder. We learn the skills of assumption identification, suspending judgment, deep listening, and asking questions of inquiry. Creating this space takes time and practice for it runs counter to our culture. Space is made for silence, for only in silence can we hear the deeper inner wisdom.

Since I have trained with Parker Palmer in his formation work, my own work with story has been deeply validated and enlarged. His work invites shared stories in many settings, as his basic belief is, "We Teach Who We Are" and "We Lead Who We Are." Learning to hold a sacred space where the soul and role of an individual intersects is at the heart of his work. Identity and integrity are critical factors in owning our stories. They are the subtle dimensions of the life long process of self-discovery.

Our greatest art

So what have I learned from 30 years of story work? I have learned the vastness of the inner world and the importance of knowing and understanding that world. Our inner world is always affecting the world around us. The world around us is always affecting the world within. We cannot separate our inner and outer reality. Story, our story, is our greatest art piece. Distilling the power and potential in our own story is life work. Stories open our hearts and connect us with the hearts of others. It behooves us to spend time knowing our story, for it influences our homes, our educational institutions, our hospitals, and our businesses: Who we are speaks more clearly than what we say, "We lead who we are." Story writing and sharing invites us to live more fully the life that wants to live in us.

Seeking Our Creative Genius

Wendy Bjornson, MPH

Wendy Bjornson is a teacher, counselor, and public health professional who, for the last 13 years, has divided her time between teaching and counseling women for personal growth and development and directing projects to benefit public health. After receiving her graduate degree and practicing public health for several years, Wendy began to see how our health issues reflect our inner nature and that women especially were searching for more meaning as they sought to improve their health. That observation, together with her personal experience led Wendy to immerse herself in the emerging fields of mind-body and energetic health and to work more closely with women. Wendy is a Certified Interactive Imagery Guide[SM] and an ordained minister trained in spiritual counseling. Her training also includes intuition development, energetic healing, and dreams.

Wendy has facilitated many groups on health changes and spiritual growth, published numerous articles on public health, conducted training for hundreds of health care providers, directed large public health projects, and has been a speaker at national and international conferences on public health and mind/body/spirit issues.

Wendy founded the Center for Creative Health as a resource center to help women develop their creative and intuitive abilities, to foster women's health and well-being, and to assist women to discover their particular genius for seeking new pathways in their lives.

Wendy Bjornson
Center for Creative Health
(503) 245-5924
(503) 892-3125 fax
createhealth@mindspring.com
www.centerforcreativehealth.net

My Story

These are extraordinary times. We find ourselves at a historic crossroads, buffeted by social and political changes so unprecedented that no one can clearly point the way. As our culture struggles to find some agreement on direction, we are faced with decisions we cannot easily make. There is no better example of our uncertainty than the presidential election of 2000, in which the decision was ultimately made in the courts and came down to a handful of votes. How will we find our way through the 21st century when so much of what we know no longer works?

There is another way. Within the U.S. and across the world, a movement that has been underway for decades is gradually evolving alternatives. Although we cannot quite bring it into focus, this movement is transforming health care, education, psychology, families and friendships, business, and the practice of our spiritual beliefs. The forces behind this movement are values that lead to respect for human and natural diversity, compassion for the plight of one another and the planet, and a desire for greater openness, warmth, and peace in our daily lives. These are values most commonly regarded as feminine. Not surprisingly, women have been the primary leaders. Today, as 40 million American women reach their creative midlife years, the pace of transformation continues to increase.

Today, more and more women are inspired to seek something they sense is real and important, but has yet to be fully expressed. I believe that what women are seeking is their inherent creative genius. I also believe that, because the vitality of women's spirits has been subverted for so long, many women are afraid to trust the energy they feel as a positive, guiding force in their lives. We need to learn how to embrace the feminine energy that is inspiring our lives and allow it to help guide us toward a more positive future.

Searching for a life of my own

I have heard women's extraordinary stories of spiritual discovery, personal accomplishment, commitment, and dedication. The feminine energy present in the lives of these women is obvious and inspiring. But the stories of these women's lives were not part of my upbringing in a small Midwestern town where traditional values were respected, the subservient role of women was considered normal, and the rules for being "nice" were carefully drawn.

As an adolescent, I complained about the role of women and was reminded that this was the way it had always been and this is the way it would always be. The obvious implication was that I should just get used to it. But I couldn't stop wondering: How is it possible for half of humanity to be so diminished in the eyes of God? Don't women have a more important place in the Universe?

Lacking guidance from others to help me find another direction, I tried to stay within the dominant beliefs of my family. Education was considered important, so I started college and wanted to become a musician. I had studied music in high school and loved both the skill it demanded and the sheer joy of creating beautiful sound. Some of my early peak life experiences were in the music listening lab and rehearsal hall surrounded by the genius of the world's most gifted composers. But I had no idea about how this passion could be part of my "real" life.

I married young, began raising a family, surrendered my dreams of being a concert musician (too impractical), and finished my training in music education instead. But my heart wasn't into teaching, jobs were scarce, and I needed to help support my family. I found a job working on a public health research project that I found interesting, and it provided a stable income.

On the outside, I had established a life I felt was expected of me, and I did love my children. But, on the inside, I had lost my creative vitality. I didn't realize how numb I felt until, one day, a friend asked me if I were taking Valium. That was the jolt I needed. I realized I had sacrificed the life I had dreamed about in order to fit myself into the life I had. In my deepest intuition, I believed that the only way I would ever find the life I sought was by creating it myself. It was an inspired thought, but I had little idea about how it could happen. I had not yet learned that my intuition could actually be trusted to help lead me there. Unable now to fit back into my marriage, I divorced and faced the prospect of creating a life that could express who I was while being responsible for raising two children.

I entered graduate school and received a degree in public health education. I gradually started to feel a sense of a new direction forming as I began to meet women with more independent lives. I thought about moving away from the Midwest and starting over. I wanted my life to be more creative, more expressive.

At the same time, I began corresponding with a male friend I had known since college who was living on the West Coast. As he became more serious, I became more skeptical. I wanted to pursue my own life. Faced with a decision about whether I should choose a future with a partner who seemed to understand what I was seeking, or a future on my own, I encouraged him to move to the Midwest so together we could decide what to do.

My intuition flashed a warning: I felt hesitant and ambivalent. Neither decision felt right, but I was too influenced by the urgency and too unsure of myself to seek my own way. We decided to marry. Within a few months, I realized that my intuition had been trying to guide me to wait. Should I have trusted my instincts and let life unfold in my own way? But now I was committed to a different path. And even though we faced many problems, we were excited about the future and believed we would find our way together.

Taking a new direction

A couple of years later, I picked up a phone message in my office from a professor in Oregon. She had called on the recommendation of a mutual friend. I felt a shiver when I looked at the number and the message asking me to return the call. I knew this was going to be a new opportunity, a chance to start over — again. After several interviews, I accepted a position. We moved West. I was finally released from the rules of being "nice."

Once settled, many problems resurfaced, and I began to dream about trying once again to find my own life. Unwilling to fail at marriage a second time, I turned instead toward finding new spiritual experiences that could enrich the life I had. I began to explore women's spirituality and mind-body health, participating in women's groups, started asking deeper spiritual questions, studied dreams, and kept a journal. As my inner life expanded, I found a sweat lodge — a Native American ceremony of purification, healing, and deep spiritual insight. I began to embrace beliefs that spiritually honored both men and women and all of nature.

These spiritual experiences threw open an inner door, giving me the guidance that had been weaving in and out of my life an open and direct channel. But now my inner guidance began seriously interfering with my real life, so I sought therapy to sort out the chaos. In therapy, I was asked to write down all the parts of my life I believed needed sorting out and what they meant to me. Intuitively, I recalled something I had written earlier in my journal.

As I began to reread, I was surprised to see, for the first time, the two voices I had so often heard in my heart. One voice was what I thought of as my "real" voice, the one I heard all the time. But the other voice seemed much clearer. As I kept reading, I recognized it as the voice of my inner guidance telling me, in my own handwriting, who I really was. I had been living my life backward! I had believed that my "real" life was most important and that my inner life was separate. I finally understood that my inner life **was** my real life and that nothing was separate.

After all the crises, I had finally gotten the message right. But now who was I going to become? Would I have to leave everything I knew? And deep within was a haunting knowledge of women generations before who had lived from their inner wisdom and were tortured and murdered. Where was I headed?

I continued with therapy but was increasingly miserable in my "real" life. Believing I still didn't know what to do, I woke up one morning shaken from a dream. The dream was short and simple, consisting only of a message: "Change your life or die." I got it. Unwilling to die, I started over once again, learning how to live guided by my inner wisdom.

I would like to say that I rose to the challenge with courage and grace. Although there were those moments, there were also many times that I doubted every step. But now I knew that, if I sincerely asked for guidance, I would find an answer. I began lengthy preparations for a vision quest: a four-day ceremony of fasting and prayer intended to help me find a vision of my purpose in life. When the ceremony was over, my life was profoundly changed. I had found my answer, and I had found myself.

The forces that so persistently kept disrupting my life were the forces of feminine energy penetrating all of our lives, helping us to seek a different way. I had been guided to find my own way, at times very painfully, in order to better serve my own life's purpose and to assist others as they seek theirs. I was finally ready to reshape my life and my career. I finished raising my children and followed my intuition as it led me to explore new professional areas and to delve deeper into the mystery of my spiritual life. I studied and became certified in Interactive Guided Imagery. I became a minister, trained in spiritual counseling, and studied energetic healing.

The most magical part of my new life was being drawn, in the mysterious way of the Universe, to the one person who would become my life's true partner, who would honor and love who I am, and who would share my spiritual life. This complete affirmation from the Universe has finally taught me to listen to my inner guidance every day and trust it to guide my life.

Seeking Our Creative Genius

The genius in every woman

I learned through one life crisis after another that the voice of the feminine speaks to everyone, not just to me. And this powerful, untiring presence seeks to move each of us toward the life that serves our highest good. Rather than being a force that seeks to destroy, this is the force that seeks to create. This voice is also becoming more insistent as the pace of our lives accelerates. The creative genius of women has not yet been fully expressed and is needed now to help illuminate the way into the future.

There is much that needs to be done before women can fully express their creative genius. We all need to learn to listen and trust our intuitive guidance, to face and overcome the inevitable obstacles, and to allow our guidance to shape our lives. But there are still many layers of uncertainty, of culturally limiting beliefs, and of fear that prevent women from opening to their genius. Although women's lives have changed a lot since I grew up, the vitality of women's creative energy has been subverted for so long, it takes a great deal of courage for many women even to begin.

The language of our intuitive guidance is simple and direct. It can come as a still, small voice, an instinctive action, a physical sensation, a flash of creativity, or a moment when you feel one with the world. When you experience intuition, you suddenly know something without analysis: the knowledge is just there. Webster's dictionary calls intuition "the immediate knowing or learning of something without the conscious use of reasoning." Intuition is direct knowledge: it tells you what to do.

Signals usually alert us to the presence of our guidance. Your spine might tingle, or you might feel a shiver. You might feel a warmth or pressure over your heart, butterflies in your stomach, or simply a sense that things are "not right." Many women describe their guidance as a feeling of an inner strength, a sense of knowing, or that something just feels right. Intuitive guidance is neutral, independent of emotion. It does not make moral judgments. It is only there to guide you to your highest purpose. Our inner guidance is always present, providing a steady stream of information, whether we pay attention or not. But, as I discovered, if you ignore it too long, it will make you listen. Your life will be disrupted by one crisis after another until you align yourself with your life's purpose. Many of us will only pay attention when we have a crisis. But we can learn to pay attention every day, allowing our guidance to help us recover from and even prevent crises.

I was very stubborn about listening to my intuitive guidance. But my intuition was persistent and powerful. Even so, it could not lead me to my highest purpose until I was also willing to face the obstacles I found along the way. Like many people, I hesitated or even took another route because I was afraid of what would happen or because I was told that I was wrong. Often it took a bigger perspective to step outside of myself.

I know now how important it is for women to learn how to listen to and trust their guidance. Because we live with a legacy of repression and fear that still permeates our beliefs, we need to learn to believe in our greatness, not our limits.

When we open ourselves and listen to our inner guidance, learn to trust its message, and become skilled at overcoming obstacles, then we can actively participate in creating a more positive future, joining our unique perspective and insight with those of others. As we create a more positive future for ourselves, we collectively create a more positive future for everyone.

At the heart of this creative process is the expression of our genius as it flows through the decisions and activities of our everyday lives. Every time we make a health decision that includes our intuitive guidance, we benefit our health, we teach those around us (including our health care providers), and we become a force for change in health care. When we allow our intuitive guidance to help us decide how to raise our children, we strengthen our relationships and teach them how to trust themselves. As we bring the full force of our passion and integrity to the causes we believe in, the world cannot help but change.

Embracing the future

On my 50th birthday, I made a commitment to use what I had learned to help awaken the force of the feminine in the lives of women, in order to inspire each of us to create a more positive future for ourselves, for our families, and for our communities. Through my own experience and the experiences of clients, friends, and even strangers, I know that this powerful feminine energy is real. I have seen that, as we align our intentions with the force of this energy, anything is possible.

I use several approaches to help women seek their genius.

- I use Interactive Guided Imagery to help women listen to specific messages from their intuitive guidance. Because intuition communicates in images, sensations, and insights, we can ask our intuition to take a form that we can understand and then create a dialogue with the form to help understand its message. This approach works for any symptom or experience we have. It is especially effective when we ask our inner guidance to take the form of an inner guide. Like a trusted friend and wise teacher, our inner guide can provide accurate advice on every aspect of our life. We only need to ask and trust the response.

- As a spiritual counselor, I help women align themselves with their higher purpose. Intuitive guidance is personal, helping us with the problems and circumstances of our everyday lives. It is also spiritual, helping us understand how we are a unique part of the Universe with a particular purpose. The spiritual counseling process assists women in their relationship with their personal life and their spiritual existence, helping them to recognize, as I eventually did, that they are one and the same.

- As an energetic healer, I help women clear and balance their energy, freeing up more energy to seek the life they want. Our bodies are surrounded and supported by energy fields. These energy fields are also how we receive and process intuitive information. Whenever a trauma occurs, large or small, it is held as a "high-voltage" memory in our energy field. When we encounter a related experience in the future, these high-voltage memories are recalled, and we experience our anxiety or fear all over again. These memories create a lot of interference in our lives. Energetic healing works by reducing the voltage in these memories so that they no longer interfere. Energetic healing helps us overcome emotional obstacles that keep us from expressing our creative genius.

These are extraordinary times. The most eloquent and diverse voices for change are coming from women. But we all need to be willing to step forward and offer our genius. We cannot wait until we know where we are headed before we speak. More than at any other time in our history, it is in the speaking that we will find our way.

Wendy Bjornson

The most important gift I discovered throughout my entire search, the answer I received after four days of fasting and prayer, was that **all women are extraordinary.** As we seek to dissolve the myth of our inferiority, as we gently reveal our creative genius, the radiance of our feminine spirit becomes dazzling. Believe that it is possible, and it is so.

Freeing the Heart

Naomi Mallinson

Naomi Mallinson is a speaker, writer, and poet with a vivid love of life and a stirring message. An honors graduate of Harvard, she sojourned for 25 years in the world of corporate data processing. *Marquis' Who's Who of American Women* published a summary of her accomplishments in computer programming, systems analysis, and data base design.

Seeking greater fulfillment, Naomi left the technical arena. Her path led to the School of Healing Arts in San Diego, where she became one of the few grandmothers to complete the Holistic Health Practitioner program. In her healing practice, she developed original forms of transformational bodywork. Using these techniques to free up the flow of vital energy, Naomi discovered she could accelerate her clients' process of self-discovery and evolution.

Spurred by a vision of a more conscious and harmonious society, Naomi redirected her career focus in 2000. As an inspirational speaker and writer, she addresses diverse audiences of highly motivated people — men and women who have attained a strong degree of effectiveness and are seeking to move to their next level.

Naomi Mallinson

By stirring the hearts of her listeners and readers, Naomi calls forth their deepest inner resources, empowering them to bridge the chasm between where they are and where they are heading.

Naomi Mallinson
Sandpiper Communications
PO Box 1801
La Mesa, CA 91944-1801
(619) 668-1060
http://home.earthlink.net/~surefooted1
surefooted1@earthlink.net

My Story

One night three years ago, I drifted into a dreamy reverie. In my mind's eye a golden bow appeared, hovering in the sky. Slowly and deliberately the bow flexed, drawn back by some invisible archer. "Oh," I cried, "It's Cupid! He hasn't forgotten me." At 53, I had married and divorced twice. The vision of the golden bow surprised and moved me.

Cupid's arrow flew. Within a few months I entered into a remarkable relationship — wondrously playful, passionate, and tender. Before long I was lost in a field of daisies! "He loves me, he loves me not, he loves me, he...." For a year and a half, I urgently queried the daisies, all the while turning a deaf ear to their replies.

I built myself a castle in the air — a dream home for the life we would share forever — but the castle had no foundation on the ground. Finally I came to recognize the truth and saw that the relationship was heading nowhere. My fragile world shattered. The future, once full of promise, now held no hope.

I sank into a tenacious depression. Seasons passed, leaden with despair. The persistent gloom took a toll on me. My lean, fit, 108-pound body withered in the course of a year to an 88-pound wraith with barely any vitality. Clearly I could not go on cursing my fate and railing against life — not if I wanted to keep body and soul together. The time had come. I needed to pick myself up, brush off the dust and carry on.

Starting Over

How does a sonnet begin, and end?
Where, on its way, does a river wend?
All the forests must shed their leaves
when the time arrives, and no one grieves.
The only thing for a heart to do
is sit right down and tie a shoe
right snug upon each foot, and then
begin the journey once again.

Tentatively I began the journey, wondering where the road ahead would lead. As I walked along, I kept looking for road signs — something like "Renewed lease on life, right lane." To my dismay the road remained utterly unmarked. I would have given anything for a compass and a map.

If only I had a sense of direction! I searched for clues. I figured it would be a good idea to discover what I cared about, what really mattered to me. To find that out, I had to allow myself to feel. Feeling brought with it intense pain, sometimes exhaustion, as my remaining grief and sorrow surfaced. Nevertheless, I ventured again and again into the hidden recesses of my heart.

Persistence paid. I identified the things that mattered to me. I discovered that I still loved life! I cared about restoring my health and regaining strength. I cherished my two grown children and my young granddaughter. I wanted to be around to nurture them and enjoy them. I wanted to inspire and encourage others through speaking and writing. The uplifting poetry I had written lay gathering dust, and I yearned to make it available to all the people who might benefit from it.

At last I had a sense of direction. Armed with a compass and a map, I could now move forward with purpose. I added a program of gentle exercise to my daily routine — and stuck with it! I practiced expressing my genuine feelings and communicating my love, especially with my family. I dropped my former mask of aloof indifference. To follow my dream of speaking and writing, I joined the National Speakers Association as an apprentice. There I met many successful speakers and authors and began to learn the ropes.

In pursuing my career goals, I often felt audacious — even foolish — to be seeking a foothold in the world of professional speaking and writing. Given my frail health and limited financial resources, how could I reasonably expect to succeed? The voice of doubt grumbled, but the voice of intuition gave me hope. Perhaps I could connect with a team of collaborators. By combining our resources, efforts, and talents, we could go far.

Continuing to trust my heart and take steps toward my goal, I attended a two-day professional development conference of the National Speakers Association. There I encountered Nancy Buhl and learned of a book project in progress — the one for this very book. Within a matter of days, I joined the team of coauthors, and my collaboration dream came true!

Freeing the Heart

The heart — the physical heart — is one of our most vital organs. In our society more people die of heart attacks and heart-related illness than any other cause. This is no coincidence. The physical heart is closely associated with the heart of poetry and love songs. That poetic heart is tender, exquisitely sensitive. The society around us is often rough, even brutal. Early in life, as small children, we begin to build protective walls as a buffer around the tender heart within us. These protective walls clamp down on the flow of vital energy to the physical heart.

We build these walls in an unconscious imitation of the similar walls we notice in our family members. The walls serve a useful purpose for us. By reducing our sensitivity to harshness, they enable us to function in our families, schools, and workplaces without collapsing or exploding in emotional distress. The walls around the heart serve as an anesthetic.

Just like many pharmaceutical anesthetics, the walls around the heart have side effects. A tiny bit of an anesthetic drug produces numbness. A little bit more produces unconsciousness, and a smidgen more brings death. That's why surgical anesthesiologists are so thoroughly trained and highly paid.

Our defensive walls around the heart act in the very same way. A little bit is numbing. We lose awareness of our feelings. The boss can insult us, and we do not notice the flood of anger that wells up inside us. A little more defensiveness brings unconsciousness. We lose awareness of our own most deeply held values, such as the love of life. As a result we become subject to devastating addictions and other destructive behaviors. Smoking, drug addiction, and alcoholism are some common examples. The ultimate side effect of our defenses is death itself. The physical heart sustains too much damage to go on functioning. It dies in a room without windows — a stagnant prison of our own devising.

At first glance, this looks like quite an awful kettle of fish. We need our defenses in order to function in society, but those same defenses rob us of life. They not only hasten our actual death, but also diminish our experience of aliveness while we live.

Fortunately, we do not need to remain in the grips of this ghastly dilemma. We have the option of choosing new, healthier ways to maintain our composure. With persistence, patience, and clear purpose, we can dismantle those protective walls and free our heart.

The three arenas of freedom

Freeing the heart takes place in three distinct arenas of life. The first is the personal arena, the stage on which you play out the drama of your life as an individual. The second is the public arena, where your actions and attitudes influence the community and society you live in. The third, the spiritual arena, is the temple within you where you sense the sacredness of creation.

- In the personal arena, freeing the heart means coming more fully alive. You rediscover who you are in your essential nature, underneath the veneer of social conditioning. You reclaim your original sparkle and spontaneity. You step off the treadmill and onto a garden path.

- In the public arena, you touch the hearts of others. Your growing freedom and freshness remind people of their own capacity for aliveness. You set an example that inspires, uplifts, and educates, helping others to grow.

- In the spiritual arena, you expand in consciousness, becoming aware of yourself at the deepest levels of being. You unite with your soul. Your delight in living takes on new dimensions, and your fulfillment no longer depends on accomplishment, status, or circumstances.

The personal arena

In the personal arena, the first thing you notice as you free your heart is that you feel so much more alive. You begin to loosen up, lighten up, and live it up!

Coming Alive!

Get in your body, sink your roots.
You and life are in cahoots!
No need to worry,
start to scurry!
The logic will follow.
No need to swallow
anything you don't desire.
Live your life alit with fire!

Notice the strong rhythm in this poem. The words acquired rhythm by passing through my heart on their way out. The heart has rhythm in spades, and wisdom too! In fact, wisdom is simply the knowing that opens to you when you connect with your heart.

Let's take a look at some of the heart's wisdom in this poem. Most of it — about 90% — hovers invisibly between the lines. It's actually embedded in the rhythm, the sound of the words, and the countless symbolic associations carried by each phrase. This wisdom is beyond the scope of the intellect. You could analyze and dissect the poem till the cows come home and never capture it. It cannot be captured by the mind, only embraced by the heart. That's how poetry reaches so deeply and communicates so powerfully — it speaks directly to the heart.

Some of the wisdom — the other 10% — presents itself in a more straightforward way. This part speaks to the mind. For example, the mind can grasp the notion that "You and life are in cahoots!" That line informs you that in the game of life, the cards are stacked in your favor. Providence takes action on your behalf.

The mind also comprehends the statement "No need to swallow anything you don't desire." That's like the time I was 6 years old and my mother served spinach. I didn't want any. It tasted awful! But I wasn't allowed to leave the table until it was gone. I sat and sat. Every time my mother left the room, I hid another glob of spinach under the plate. After a while it was "all gone" and I left the table with a clean plate, a clean conscience, and an impish gleam in my eye.

The public arena

Your heart has a cadence and a rhythm, a music all its own. This music emanates from you and reverberates all around you. On a subtle level, the music of your heart influences the hearts of others. As you progress in freeing your heart, the music you emanate grows stronger, more harmonious, and more lively. Other hearts hear it and begin to sway to your music. As more and more people awaken, each becoming a center of wholesome influence for those around them, the whole earth benefits.

Naomi Mallinson

African Drum

The living earth's heart beats true.
Conscious islands are too few!
Ignite the souls in many men,
multiply the horde by ten.
Sing a tune of heart's own fire,
play upon a minstrel's lyre.
Lead the way to kingdom come.
Beat upon an African drum
deep inside the soul of you.
Rise and shine, and follow through.

The follow through is important. As you grow in awareness, you gain a greater and greater capacity to make a positive difference in the world. You outgrow your previous roles and ways of contributing. Life then promotes you and offers you a "job" at a higher level of responsibility. The pay goes up as well, in terms of fulfillment and joy. Step forward with confidence into your new role, even if it feels uncomfortable or intimidating. Remember, you and life are in cahoots! Life will provide you with ample on-the-job training.

The spiritual arena

The heart is the seat of courage. With a free heart, you dare to delight. You question musty old rules and explore enticing new byways. You remember how to play. You burst into song while doing the dishes or driving on the freeway. Laughter wells up from your spirit and spills out all over!

Your relationship to the Creator also changes. You notice the sacred aspect of nature more often and more distinctly. Your spiritual feelings take on a rapturous quality rather than a solemn one.

Psalm of the Seven "Sins": Pleasure, Gladness, Mischief, Play, Questioning, Exploring, Laughter

Mirth twinkles in my eyes, oh Lord,
and runs down through the soles of my feet
and into thy hallowed ground.
Playgrounds unfold in the mist of dawn skies.

Jungle Gyms. Meta-stairways.
Living sparkling flywheels of brilliant color.
Majestic skies and singing mountains.
Take my feet and dance them, Lord.
Pray me to the top of the steeple.
Set me down in green pastures
with the wildflowers and the bees.
Give me the fire of laughter deep in my belly.
Roll me over and over down the slopes,
careening in free fall.
Cascade me over the waterfall
and into the swirling River of thy streaming.

When you begin to experience rapture, your creative works take on a whole new character. Poetry flows more freely and sings more sweetly. Painting becomes more vivid and luminous. Drawing becomes more spontaneous, and pictures emerge onto paper of their own volition. Your creative expression now comes from a deeper place in you, the level of spirit.

Five helpful practices

Five simple practices can help you in the process of freeing your heart. Explore these pathways with a sense of fun and adventure. You'll spark the growth of spontaneity and add richness to your daily life.

1. Give enjoyment priority.

We've all been taught to keep our nose to the grindstone. We try to get all the "important" things done before we allow ourselves to indulge in fun. In truth, fun and enjoyment are way more important than most of the stale dry tasks that consume our days and weeks. Give enjoyment priority and make sure you get your daily quota.

2. Notice beauty and goodness.

The heart delights in beauty and appreciates every form of goodness. Make a habit of noticing beauty — the tree branches blowing in the wind, the glint of golden sunlight in the late afternoon, the dimple in your little girl's smile. Also notice the goodness that comes your way — the courteous driver who slows

Naomi Mallinson

down to let you change lanes, the stranger who pauses to hold a door open for you, the caring telephone call from a friend.

3. Engage in rhythmic movement.

Your heart revels in rhythmic movement. That's why it feels so good to clap your hands when you sing or listen to music. Fill your days with cheerful rhythm! If you're waiting on hold on the telephone, hum a little tune and snap your fingers. Try out various forms of dance or improvise your own. Enjoy a brisk walk or a leisurely stroll. Any simple rhythmic movement can lift your spirits when you are down, and bring you back to the ease and simplicity of the present moment. A heavy heart comes from dwelling on miseries of the past or potential problems in the future. Lighten up by living in the here and now.

4. Pay attention to your hunches.

The mind analyzes, the heart feels. Hunches are feelings that arise from within you, like the slight uneasiness you feel in your stomach when you are about to shortchange yourself or someone else. Some hunches say, "Uh-oh!" and others say, "Oh boy!" Paying attention to these subtle feelings is an easy and rewarding way to listen to your heart.

5. Discover and use your creative gifts.

As a small child you were a consummate artist. You hadn't yet learned there was a "right" way to paint, draw, sculpt, sing, or dance — you just did it. Set aside your inhibitions and experiment. Find out what kinds of creative expression you most enjoy and spend time on those. Your pictures, poems, or songs don't have to be "good" — just genuine, heartfelt and satisfying.

Follow your heart

As you dismantle those old protective walls and free your heart, you discover what it is that you care about most deeply. You feel your own passion and longing, your heart's desire. Pay attention, and dare to follow your heart. Your heart is the wisest part of you and will never lead you astray.

— 158 —

Heart's Desire

The trailing question still remains:
What dost thou want from earth to take?
If nothing lurketh in the heart,
it matters little where to start.

I see a small and rambling brook.
Around the bend I peer and look.
It seemeth like a little book
of rhymes and whimsies and a cook
that flips the flapjacks down
and turns around the sour frown.

I see a puppy and it squirms
and wriggles — not from worms,
but with a spirit oh so bright —
and walks about without no fright!

The mysteries and red balloons
go hand in hand with Mistress Moon,
and muddy pies and cakes galore
await you by a handyman's door.

I see an old and rustic gate
and on it, with a head of state,
the smile of Jefferson's bust to seem
a miracle of the American dream.

The truest home lies deep inside
and when the groom and the blushing bride
come home to find the love life there,
the rest around them comes to bear.

I see a free wheeling real estate
with all the acres — up to eight —
and on them me and Mistress May
and all the kin who come to stay.

Naomi Mallinson

Wherever land and sea come from,
I long to lie in the noon day sun
and count the blessings and the sheep,
and carry them to memories deep
of love and golden dawns and days,
and bring them forth in novel ways.

The straw hats and the circus clowns,
and all the children upside down
and sideways in the mirror now
do come and take a little bow
and cover up their smallness with
a smile so big it takes the breath
to newer heights and mocketh death.

Transform Life-Threatening Events into Life-Affirming Soul Growth

Monica D. Traystman, PhD

Monica D. Traystman, PhD, is President of Healthy Spirit, Inc., a wellness company that develops and presents seminars, workshops, and retreats to promote and maintain a balanced mind, body, and spirit. Educational programs in the areas of health, wellness, and complementary/ integrative medicine are designed for an individual's personal and professional well-being. These programs can be presented in small group, corporate, and community group settings.

Her company provides these types of individual and group services: Spiritual wellness consultations, Primordial Sound Meditation classes, Tools for Effective Living classes, yoga, Embody-ment yoga therapy, heated stone therapy, self-esteem sessions, and Reiki sessions.

A scientist by academic training, Monica received a BA in Biology from St. Andrews Presbyterian College, an MS in Psychometrics from The Johns Hopkins University, a doctorate from The Johns Hopkins School of Hygiene and Public Health, and she completed her postdoctoral fellowship in Human Molecular

Genetics at The Johns Hopkins Hospital. Following her training she was an Assistant Professor in the Department of Pathology and Microbiology at the University of Nebraska Medical Center. And then in 1999 her career and her life took a startling turn toward integration of spirituality and complementary/alternative medicine.

Monica has been certified as a Primordial Sound meditation instructor by Drs. Deepak Chopra and David Simon at The Chopra Center for well-being, La Jolla, Calif.; certified as a Reiki Master by Joyce Swanson; certified by Jack Canfield, co-author of *Chicken Soup for the Soul* book series, as a Self-Esteem and Peak Performance seminar facilitator; certified by Rama Berch, Founder and Director, Master Yoga Academy, to teach Hatha yoga in the Svaroopa style; and she is a registered Yoga Alliance teacher. Monica is continuing her yoga studies to become a yoga therapist. She is also studying to become a Western astrologer with Linda Brady (Baltimore, MD) and a Jyotish (Vedic) astrologer with Marc Boney and Brent BecVar (La Jolla, CA).

Monica D. Traystman, PhD
President
Healthy Spirit, Inc.
La Jolla, CA
www.iamahealthyspirit.com

My Story

The unbelievable reality of having the opportunity of dying three times in this lifetime was hard for me to comprehend much less transform. Two episodes of breast cancer and a near-fatal car accident provided many life lessons from which to learn and grow. From perceiving the trees in the forest to slowly stepping back to look at the entire forest was God's plan for me to transmute negative experiences and energy to positive understanding and wisdom.

These incidents provided the opportunity for my soul growth and ultimately a deepening of my relationship with God. Experiencing and transmuting severe pain on all levels — mental, physical, emotional, and spiritual — was an act of God's love to bring me to a new understanding of compassion, self-discipline, and love for myself. This transmutation set the stage for experiencing ultimate freedom from my external experiences of life.

I want to inspire others to always have hope in their life. Playing the role of victim in my life was not something I wanted to do. Through the process of transmutation, I was led to my own truth that provided a more meaningful way to live my life. Through commitment, diligence, surrender, and love, I was able to deepen my understanding of God's plan for my life. The gifts I received from these three events launched me into my current career and prepared me for my next spiritual partnership in life. My life is a beautiful painting always in progress, always transforming.

As I walk forward in my life, I carry my inner light to share with others to empower and support them in their alchemical transformations for their life paths. My experiences offer authenticity to help you believe that whatever your experiences, the ultimate transmutation results in love. That is the only lesson of importance.

Monica D. Traystman

Transform Life-Threatening Events into Life-Affirming Soul Growth

The Alchemist

ACT 1, Scene 1

I am riding alone in a ferris wheel seat, locked in, and can't get out, no choice but to go with the flow. I am drawn up, riding backward, not knowing where I am going, but trusting that someone, somewhere, is guiding my journey. Hurled upward, my stomach flies into my throat, my seat swings and I am so scared. What will I find? How bad can the worst answer be? Deep inside of me I already know.

The answer was there when I had the consultation. I saw the look on their faces. I heard their words, but I did not believe them. Smiling, I said, "Sure we will wait until I get to the top of the ferris wheel ride to get the answer." God has never let me down in all of the other devastating things that have happened to me. Yes, maybe there is an outside chance of a miracle. Of course, a miracle! That's my answer!

"Monica, you are all right. You came through like a trooper. Your surgery was very successful, and your recovery will go well. I had to remove your left breast, and we took some nodes to check things out. Did you hear me? Do you understand what I just said?"

The voice was that of my wonderful surgeon. I lay there thinking this is a movie and his voice is so grounded and reassuring. So, I really did have breast cancer. Well right now that soothing voice made me feel as if this news was some sort of superficial message banner one sees flying behind the tail of a small plane at the beach. At first you hear it, then you see it, and then it goes away never to be seen again.

I closed my eyes to sink down into the lovely comfort of the anesthetic cloud that held me in its arms protecting me from the cruel world that wanted to take a body part. I would be all right! It was February 1973.

Here I was, 27 years old, married for a year and a half and no history of breast cancer in my family. This didn't make any sense to me. The big question kept reeling through my mind: Why?

I was afraid to move, afraid to breathe, afraid to touch the beautiful place on my body that now had a wound. I knew the reality of what had happened. I just didn't want it to come alive. Does anybody know who I am and how I feel? I have just lost a part of my body. Who will love me now? Will I die?

All I could see from my hospital window was a small piece of cloudy sky, a reflection of glare and old red brick buildings. I am still alive even though I am encased like a mummy who has lost her femininity in layers of gauze and heavy surgical tape. It's like a rebirth.

I have been birthed into a new life as a person who wears an old costume that has been refitted by the dresser but who has a new part to play in the soap opera of life.

ACT 1, Scene 2

"Yes, I am very hungry today. Aren't you?" I smiled at my friend as we walked down the hall toward our offices with big containers filled with salads from the hospital cafeteria. I was feeling great this day in May 1982 having just completed my annual medical exams with flying colors. Proud I had gotten past the five-year mark to beat the statistics and then the seven-year mark where I could actually say in a whisper, "I had breast cancer." Now I had the goal to make 10 years and beyond! I was going to be the finest role model, showing every woman that you could survive breast cancer!

"Hi, Monica," said the chief of surgery, stopping to talk to me.

My inner knowing said, "Uh oh, something does not feel good. I don't like this."

My surgeon looked at me with his friendly, penetrating eyes and calmly said, "I need to see you and your husband in my office. When would be the best time to make an appointment?"

My mind, body, brain, and mouth were all detached from one another. I felt myself talking but couldn't remember what I said. I felt myself halfway smile out of politeness and began to feel a warm ripple of courage from my British-Scots-Irish-German ancestry toughen up inside, readying myself for a mysterious battle. Yes, of course, a time and date. I would call his office right away after conferring with my husband.

My God, what was going to happen to me now? I have a life to live, children to birth, a husband to love, dreams to realize. No, no, not again. I had bought another ticket on the ferris wheel.

Waking up from this surgery was a snap. That was God's gift to me. Yes, this time I sailed through having another part of my body artistically removed, but the prognosis was even better. My diagnoses from both of these episodes had given me the best possible outcome. Yet another gift I was to realize later. Surely this time I was home free! The pathology report said, "All nodes negative," just like the first report.

I knew inside that this would be the end of this chapter of my life. I was going to be all right! Without a doubt I had a knowing about this. Now my body felt balanced, now I felt healthy, now I was saved from the jaws of defeat, now I could begin my next new life. My costume was re-fitted, and I was ready to arrive on stage and hear the audience applauding to announce my success.

ACT 1, Scene 3

"What is your name? Can you hear me? Where do you live? How old are you?" the voices asked.

Why are they asking me these questions? I can see them but my eyes won't open. My energy feels them. I feel so wonderful, so balanced and smooth.

Please stop asking me the same question over and over again. Yes, you are very kind, and I really appreciate everything you are doing for me. No, I don't have any family living with me here. Why are you asking me all of these personal questions?

I know those sounds. Beep, beep, beep, metal clanging, doors opening and closing. I am on a stretcher. Oh, I can't get my breath. Where are you taking me?

This all feels too real. Where is God? I was just with God. I am a little ball of golden light. I see, but don't have eyes, I feel, but don't have a body, I know but don't have a brain. My energy sits with God's energy as we converse — instantaneous transmission of information. My soul mission is still operative on earth. I am not going home. I am to go back to earth and do more work. I feel surrounded by the most fulfilling, beautiful love I have ever known. I want to stay here. Near the light, near the warmth, near the love.

Bob saw the whole thing. He was driving just behind me and tried not to crash into my sports car. It was impossible for him to stop in time. Bob, his wife, and one of his two sons were driving home from a wedding that October night in 1991. I was headed home from a local theater after seeing a play on death. In the play, death was kept up in a tree and was prevented from coming down so nobody on earth could die. Eventually death manipulated his way down and came back to "life" to continue the human cycle of life and death here on earth.

Standing in my hospital room two days after the accident, Bob asked if I remembered going into the S curve? I didn't remember but wanted to know more.

"This beat up ol' truck came barreling around the curve and smashed right into your side," Bob told me. "The truck shoved you up against the concrete barricade and totally crushed your car like an accordion. All of the glass in your car blew out. I jammed on my breaks and screeched to a halt, but I wasn't fast enough to get my car stopped. I am so, so sorry. I hit your car. I bolted out of my car when I saw your car on fire. I just knew that I had to get you out!"

"But why did you risk your life for me?" I wanted to know. "You don't even know me."

"I was divinely pushed," he said. "I could feel it. I knew I had to get to you. So, I climbed through the back window, got you out of your seat belt and pulled you out so quick I didn't have time to think about the glass. It was a miracle I didn't get cut up and all. Then the car blew up just as I got you far enough away. I didn't even stop to think about what injuries you had. Just knew I had to get you away from that burnin' car, that's all. Everyone thought you were dead. There was so much blood all over you. You had a big gash on the left side of your head. The paramedics came within five minutes and said you were alive. Held your head straight as they strapped you to the stretcher. But we couldn't get any information out of you. Did you hear anybody talkin' to you?"

"Yes, but I thought I was dreaming." So many puzzle pieces. It would take time to put them together.

I think my costume is the same. I haven't been told what the changes are. "I'll think about that tomorrow," said Scarlett O'Hara, in *Gone With the Wind.*

ACT 2

The reality of my two breast cancer events and my car accident changed my view of life in many ways. The evolution from viewing these events as a living horror story to receiving them as gifts was not done over night but involved a process of commitment, perseverance, trust, and love. Even surrounded by people along the way, I knew innately that I was to do this journey alone. There would be many facets of these events that would bring me closer to my life's purpose and therefore my soul's evolution during this lifetime.

The first big issue dealt with total release of fear that allowed this void to be filled up with a new awareness of unconditional love. Even though I felt love for myself and others all of my life, I needed to expand my conscious understanding of love through greater trust and faith as experienced through these dramatic events. I struggled with fear about why I had breast cancer on two separate occasions. I knew that I could continually seek answers that would get me nowhere and result in self-torment. But I decided to use my courage and ask someone I loved very much, my mother, to provide some potential insights.

She related to me that I had received low dose radiation to my enlarged thymus when I was 3 years old on the recommendation of two physicians. Due to a hospital fire I would not be able to check the records to verify anything pertaining to this event. I was so frozen in horror, numbness, and anger I could hardly talk. I wept and grieved so much that I wondered if I would ever recover from this insult to my life. I felt tremendous loss of control over my life due to someone else making critical decisions that affected my life drastically. Additionally, I was overwhelmed that my body may not heal and that my life would end.

Slowly over time this huge fear was replaced with trust, faith, patience, and enormous love as God brought me through a multi-level healing process. I was empowered with new strength, courage, and insights about the purpose of my life as a spiritual teacher and facilitator of healing.

The lessons of transmuting fear into love continued when I was involved in my car accident. Yet another situation I had no control over and which left me astonished as to why I had to go through another devastating event that threatened my life! From these events, I have learned that any event in my life is a gift of growth that engenders a more intimate relationship with God. The opportunity for me to gracefully receive the outcomes of these events has allowed me to see them as truly divine gifts. Each gift has included a healing experience, loving people, greater love, under-standing and compassion for others, and myself, and obtaining a higher level of consciousness through transcendence.

The second big issue resulting from these events involved developing a more intimate and stronger relationship with God. I was shocked at myself for the immense anger I felt toward God who

I had loved and honored all of my life. Playing a victim was definitely not the role I wanted to play in my precious life. I cried to exhaustion to find a decent logical answer as to why these three events and many more had happened to me. I pleaded with God to help me find the answers that would return me to a whole and balanced life.

Through another many-faceted process I again let go of more fear and replaced it with a richer understanding of unconditional love. I realized that God was asking me to change and grow beyond the box I had made for myself. This evolution would provide a stronger partnership with more clarity so that I could receive the next step in God's master plan for my soul growth toward wholeness and freedom. This step involved a greater expansion of my spiritual self, an appreciation and growth of my extrasensory gifts, and obtaining a greater depth of integration in all aspects of my life.

As I look back over time and see how carefully and with patience, support, and love God masterfully brought me out of these events, I felt myself lifted up to a new realm of being. The divine light within began to become brighter and brighter. People noticed something new about me and I thankfully appreciated their acknowledgment of this magnificent change.

Since these events I have continued to have many challenging opportunities in my life. But now I know that God must have a lot of faith in me! As quickly as God throws me a question to solve, I respond with an answer. Then just as quickly I receive another challenging question! Each day I sit at a spiritual roundtable and wait for the question(s) so I can creatively answer it. This process confirms that my soul is growing and transforming everyday in my extraordinary life!

ACT 3

I was recently introduced to a new friend who, like myself, had a most difficult health challenge over which she had no control. Her mother had been given diethylstilbestrol (DES) to prevent spontaneous abortion. As a result, a high frequency of female children develop gynecological tumors, which she did. When she related her story, we both were in tears, as we knew without speaking that we were not in control of the events that played out in our lives. But these seemingly devastating events helped us both transmute negative experiences and energy into positive, healing life journeys.

As our lives transformed we both dedicated them to the service of others. We share our authentic experiences to guide others toward believing that infinite possibilities are present each moment of our lives for healing and growth of our souls.

I am not a victim anymore. I am the victor of my life. My relationship with God is very intimate. I never wait to talk to God. Any time is the right time. I am filled with gratitude for every moment in my life. Each day I look forward to see what sacred events I can incorporate into my painting of daily life and what they will teach me. Each person who comes into my life is a sacred being, brought to me by God for a reason. Sometimes the reason is obvious and sometimes I know God has put me in the other person's life to be a part of their life lesson for the day. I am lovingly detached from the movie script as it plays out, not in a cold, distant, self-protective way but a wholesome way. In so doing, I can be more by doing less, give authentically from my heart center, and hear God's guidance more clearly.

Currently, I am exploring more healing modalities in vibrational medicine (for example, sound healing and crystal and stone healing). I believe that every thing on this planet was put here for a reason. I am trying to know and understand whatever produces positive growth and well-being and share my experiences with others.

To love is to know God and to know God is to know Love. I know God loves me and always has and always will. I am assured that one day I will rest in the comfort of God's love as I did before I was born and during my near-death experience. Even now I continue to share that love in a genuine and authentic way with every being on earth, to continue to affirm God's love in me and ultimately in my soul's evolution. That really is why I am here — to be a being of love and light. That's really why there is only love.

Finding the Gift that Adversity Brings

Donna Miesbach

Donna Miesbach was certified as a Primordial Sound Meditation instructor by Dr. Deepak Chopra at the Chopra Center for well-being in La Jolla, Calif. Donna is also a published poet and author. Currently Donna is Editor and Publisher of *Gleanings, A Bi-Monthly Discussion of Life Issues™*. Her program, *Tools for Teens™*, has found wide acceptance both here and abroad. In addition to her writing and teaching, Donna is also an inspirational speaker and offers personal enrichment workshops on a variety of topics.

Donna was one of the initial Stephen Leaders at Countryside Church in Omaha and is a retired organist and private music instructor. All of Donna's endeavors fall under the umbrella of Miesbach Associates.

Donna Miesbach
Miesbach Associates
2805 S. 161st Plaza
Omaha NE 68130
(402) 330-2474
gleanings1@juno.com

Donna Miesbach

To order:

Gleanings, A Bi-Monthly Discussion of Life Issues™. 1
yr: $7.50; 2 yrs: $12 (Gift subscriptions $5). Large print edition $9
(Gift subscriptions $7.50). International rate: 1yr: $10; 2yrs: $17.50.
Bulk rate subscriptions available upon request.

***Tools for Teens — A Course in Life Skills for People on
the Growing Edge***™. Course manual: US $24.95 + $5 shipping &
handling. Volume discounts available upon request. International
orders: $24.95 each, US currency only. Shipping to be determined at
time of purchase.

Send orders to 2805 S. 161st Plaza, Omaha, NE 68130 USA.

My Story

I will always be grateful that Neal came into my life. We were
among the fortunate few who had a truly good marriage. The down
side was his constant battle with heart disease, the many surgeries,
the frantic midnight rides to the hospital. The frequent crises
seemed to create a stark relief that pointed out with a strange sort
of clarity how deep our love was for each other.

Including our courtship, we had almost 25 years to cherish
that love. Each time trouble loomed its frightening head, Neal
seemed to be in the right place at the right time. Some new medical
miracle had always been discovered just at the time he needed it, so
of course we were thrilled that last day in May when the doctor's
call came: "These are the best numbers we've ever had! I think
we're finally getting a handle on this." That could mean a few more
years! We celebrated the happy possibility, but it was not to be.

Fourteen days later, Neal went outside to check the sprinklers
and he never came back. Even though the paramedics did all they
could to help him, this time there was no discussing it. No opportunity to pray him through the crisis. No chance to ask for another
reprieve. This time "they" had come for him, and now he was gone.

Two weeks after Neal died, my emotional dam broke and a
siege of absolute, uncontrollable sobbing set in. After about four
hours, I could hardly breathe. That's when I called my minister.

"I can't do this, Lea. I just can't do it," I wailed into the phone.

"Oh yes, you can," she answered, "and you will."

Somehow, hearing her say that, I began to wonder if it might
be possible. She had already been down this road. If she could do it,
perhaps I could, too.

Long night of the soul

Thus began my long night of the soul. I had been put on a path not of my choosing with no idea where it was going, or whether I even had the courage to walk upon it. The one saving factor was my firm belief that all things come bearing a gift. My determination to find that gift was what got me through the days and weeks that followed. Without a doubt, this was the most difficult thing I have ever had to do. To my surprise, it has also been one of the most rewarding.

Change — especially great change — can be the bearer of many lessons. One of my lessons had to do with grief itself. I always thought grief was something that happened to you, that it was an unwelcome visitor who came to stay. "Once in grief, always in grief" had been my understanding. Fortunately, I was wrong. Grief has been one of my most important teachers, but like all teachers, once the lesson is learned, you move on to an instruction of a different sort.

Another lesson had to do with the difference between pain and suffering. Pain is an inevitable part of life, but suffering is a matter of choice. We suffer when we cling to the pain. Certainly we suffer when we grieve. It's a natural part of the process, but if we are to get on with our life, at some point we need to be willing to let go of our pain. This is not to say we will forget where we have been or what we have been through. The memory will always be a vivid reminder of what has brought us to where we are.

One of the most difficult aspects of losing Neal was the huge void it left in my life. We had been so complete together, so very much at one with each other. Now he was gone. It was as though half of me was missing. It was too soon, of course, for me to know that this, too, would be one of my most important lessons.

The teacher for that lesson came along in the person of Dr. Deepak Chopra and the Primordial Sound Meditation practice he teaches. I've studied meditation nearly all my life, but this was different. This practice allowed me to reconnect with my soul. Because Primordial Sound Meditation made such a profound difference in my recovery, I eventually committed to being certified so I could share this wonderful practice with others.

Donna Miesbach

Our wholeness is within us

Through my meditation practice and through other courses Deepak offers, I began to understand that our wholeness is within us. We are not dependent on any other person or any other thing to be complete. We are infinite, eternal beings who are here for a short time to have a human experience, but we are far more than this mortal body. I'd always had a sense of that, but never so clearly as now. Finding that out moved me a bit further away from the darkness, a bit closer to the light.

As my healing progressed, I felt a growing desire to reach out in other ways to friends who were also in the grip of grief. Although my phone calls and visits were appreciated, I really wanted to do something more substantial, so *Gleanings, A Bi-Monthly Discussion of Life Issues™,* was born. Its purpose has been to uplift and encourage our readers. We talk about everything from joy to sorrow, and a lot in between. We are now in our sixth year.

Gradually the pieces were coming together. One of those pieces appeared in a form I never would have anticipated. It first came to my attention soon after Neal died when I received a letter from the Board of Christian Outreach at our church. At their meeting the night before he died, Neal had suggested offering scholarships to children from disadvantaged areas to help further their education. Although I was surprised to learn about this conversation, at some deep level I felt Neal was showing me how to use the memorial money that was coming in.

As I searched for possible scholarship candidates, I was shocked to learn what some of our young people have to do just to survive. We did give the scholarships, and while the money was certainly helpful, there was so much more these young people needed. Somehow, some way, I wished I could offer it.

As I continued the difficult business of picking up the pieces of my life, always in the back of my mind were the children. I'd read about them in the paper. I'd see them on the news. My heart would ache to see their plight, but what could I possibly do? I'm just an ordinary, average person, I'd tell myself, and a widow, at that.

Guidance in the night

The weeks grew into months, the months into years. Every time I heard another distressing story, I would pray for guidance, but nothing ever came. Finally, one night in utter frustration, I stood by the side of my bed and declared out loud, "I give up! If this isn't what You want me to do, that's fine with me. If there really is something I should be doing, You're going to have to show me what it is, because until You do, I'm not going to do a thing!" With that I turned off the light and went to bed.

At 2 A.M. I was awakened, and there in front of me were the words: *Tools for Teens — A Course in Life Skills for People on the Growing Edge.* Below it was the outline for what was to go in it. "Oh my!" was all I could think of to say.

The next morning I went straight into my office and started working on the manuscript. The gist of it centered around learning to be a responsible choice maker, about taking care of yourself, about finding healthy ways to process your emotions, and learning to tune in to your own inner wisdom.

It was evident from the start that I would need permission to use some of the material that would be in it, so I called the Chopra Center and told them what I was doing. They gave me their blessing and asked me to send them a draft once I had it all down on paper. It was a huge task, but finally, a year and a half later, we went to print. To my immense gratitude, the Chopra Center endorsed the program, and now the Tools are being taught both here and abroad in what, to me, is an amazing array of venues to people of all ages.

The past seven years have been an incredible journey, certainly one I never would have asked for. Even so, I am deeply grateful for the lessons — and yes, the gifts — it has brought into my life, not the least of which was the discovery that it is possible to move beyond our grief. Finding that out not only set my spirit free, it opened doors the likes of which I had not even dreamed.

Finding the Gift that Adversity Brings

As unwelcome as adversity may be, it does shape and define us in ways that nothing else can. The good news is that nothing is ever wasted. All things do come bearing a gift. If we are faithful to the call, we will find it really is possible to overcome "even this." How we do that is up to us. All that remains, then, is to figure out how. That "how" can be pretty overwhelming at times, but we do not walk the path alone, nor was it ever intended that we should.

There will always be dark valleys to walk through. At times we may even feel there is no way out, but there is a way out, and we will find it if we can just go with the flow and see where life is trying to take us.

Trust is an awesome tool. It brings a new dynamic into our experience and allows us to find both meaning and purpose as we encounter the truths we have been seeking.

One of the ways we find those truths is by letting go. Letting go of how things were. Letting go of how we would like things to be. Letting go of the need to try to change what we cannot change. Letting go is incremental to our healing. Until we let go, we cannot move forward. As the old saying goes, you have to put both feet in the boat before it can take you where you need to go. Letting go means putting both feet in the boat. It means accepting the lesson inherent in your situation and then moving forward on the strength of what you have learned.

Victories of the spirit require — indeed, demand — letting go of things as they were. Letting go teaches us to be comfortable with uncertainty, perhaps even learning to welcome it as a friend. It is an austere discipline, this "simple" act of letting go, and yet its rewards are generous, for through it we learn acceptance. Acceptance allows us to see what is possible. In that understanding lies the seed of our ultimate healing.

Usually when challenge comes to greet us, we put up a wall of resistance. We struggle with it, perhaps even fight against it. Although this is only natural, resistance never wins. Resistance is always in a state of battle. Acceptance leads to the way out. Acceptance allows us first of all to see things as they are. It gives us the perspective we need to see what we can or can't change. Then we are free to choose, and what we choose are our thoughts, our feelings, and our response to what is happening in our life. This means going inward to those deep places where thoughts and feelings originate, so we can consciously enter into that creative process.

Thoughts are strange creatures. They are community-oriented critters, and they tend to multiply into more of the same. Over time they cluster into patterns. They develop into habits. Before we know it, those habits end up governing our life. We become so accustomed to their sheer repetition that we just slip into automatic. While being "on automatic" does not require much actual thinking, neither does it allow us to live life consciously.

Being open to change

Becoming aware that we do have a choice in how we think and feel is the first step toward bringing our habits into the light of conscious awareness. When we aren't on automatic, it is easier to recognize when we are being given an opportunity to learn something. If we choose to focus on that lesson, we open ourselves to change — healthy change. This is important. When we change our response to life, our experience changes, too, which of course is what we wanted all along.

Although our challenges will all be different, there are some basic things you can do to make the going a little easier. At least they did for me.

For example, you might begin by looking at the patterns in your daily life. Pay attention to how you respond to what life is bringing your way. Listen to what you are thinking. Audit your feelings. It is a discipline, of course, but when you watch your inner activity much as an outside observer would, it is easier to see how you are molding and shaping your days. This frees you to work with the every day events of your life and let them be your teacher, even the events that are the most difficult — *especially* the ones that are the most difficult. Your most difficult moments are the ones that offer you the most room for growth, so try making a conscious effort to be grateful for whatever comes into your life.

That may sound pretty simple, but it is more important than you might think. Try appreciating how special each moment is. Recognize the precious opportunity inherent in each day. While you are at it, see if you can find ways to put aside some of the busyness that fills your days so you can make room to reconnect with the peace and stillness that are the very ground of your being. Then bring that stillness into your daily life, into your every thought and feeling. Day after patient day, integrate that stillness and that peace into your daily living and see the difference it makes.

If you do, you may even notice there is a presence that is always with you. The faithfulness of that presence just may open a door — a way of seeing — you've never known before. You may even begin to sense that same presence in others, too. You may see that same living, loving presence looking back at you everywhere you go. When that happens, you will know you are never really alone, no matter what. That knowing creates a confidence and fortitude that will help carry you through other difficult times.

Another important lesson is learning not to judge. We all do this. We judge things constantly. This is good, that is bad. This is happy, that is not. We like this, we don't like that. This kind of mindset is a form of resistance. When we judge, we aren't accepting things as they are. *Whenever* we resist, our inner peace is disturbed. The peace we are talking about, of course, is the peace you have found in the stillness, in the quiet presence of your soul.

If you find you are doing a lot of judging, it would be good to work on your thinking. At first it may seem like you are trying to catch a river, but if you stick with it, gradually, over time, you will begin to see a difference. It will get easier to let go. To let be what will be. To not get hung up on results. To trust that whatever happens is for the best.

We're talking about surrender, and surrender can open up a deep source of strength when the going gets rough.

You see, it really is possible to change your habits. It really is possible to direct your mind and teach it what you want it to do. This is important, because then you'll be able to draw a line beyond which you are not willing to go. You'll know when you are approaching deep water, and you'll consciously choose not to go where you do not want to swim. Instead, you'll focus on what you *do* want, so you can bring more of that quality into your experience.

Then, regardless of what else is happening in your life, you can still find some measure of happiness. You can still rest in that beautiful, loving presence you have come to know during those quiet, silent times. This kind of acceptance, this kind of freedom is very healing. It allows you to use your pain as a means of growth. It allows you to see through your challenge to one of the greatest gifts it offers — who you really are.

So day after day simply, humbly practice being who you are. In all the little daily things, affirm the truths on which you are hanging the sum total of your faith. Then you'll begin to understand that your thoughts, your life, and even your death are just stages in your journey. You'll know for yourself that there is no darkness. There is only light, and it is everywhere. More and more, you'll begin to see that the fabric of your life is one uncut, unbroken whole. More than that, now you'll know that you are whole, regardless of what else may be going on. This is the ultimate healing of which we spoke. In that moment of silent understanding, all your fears just slip away as quietly as they came.

Be Still

Be still, my soul
   and question not
The unseen hand
   that wrought the plot
That brought you to
   this time and place,
For all your doubts
   will not erase
The things that made you
   what you are
And brought you to
   this very hour,
So do not strain
   or question why.
The stars are in their place —
   and so am I!

Donna Miesbach

Angel Flight ~ A Journey of Choice

Nancy Buhl

In her lifelong quest of self-exploration, self-improvement, and soul searching for the meaning of life, Nancy Buhl has achieved the equivalent of a PhD, embracing and celebrating life's lessons of trials and tribulations. She opens her heart to discuss a journey of questioning her right to live when her 19-year-old brother passed away.

Her triumph over a childhood fear was celebrated in her 40s when she joined Toastmasters International. The achievement of Distinguished Toastmaster and Area Governor of the Year of Founder's District laid the foundation for the most rewarding blessings of conducting Youth Leadership Programs. Her passion for youth was expanded by participation in the Mentoring Council of Pasadena, the first city in California to achieve the distinction of a Mentoring City, through the California Governor's Initiative.

A graduate of the Anthony J. Robbins' Life Mastery University and Trainer Academy furthered her quest. Membership in the Greater Los Angeles Chapter of the National Speakers Association and pursuit of a BA degree from the American College of

Nancy Buhl

Metaphysical Theology enables her to steer a course of embracing and sharing life lessons. She describes a self-fulfilling prophecy, which resulted in a car accident at the age of 21, ending a lifelong dream of being a professional dancer.

Last, but certainly not least, she embraces a victorious celebration of thriving beyond a diagnosis of breast cancer, surgery, and radiation treatments at the Kaiser Permanente Los Angeles Medical Center. Her mission of caring and sharing was once again demonstrated with participation in a quality improvement program for patients and caregivers, serving as a reminder of the divine tapestry connecting each one of us in a dance of spiritual evolution.

"Touched by an Angel" is often how others refer to Nancy, who shines as a beacon of love, understanding, and compassion. With visionary insight and an attitude of gratitude, she inspires others to embrace their life, challenges, and lessons and to celebrate their unique talents, gifts, and divinity.

This journey of trials and tribulations is dedicated to her mom, Dorothy Mullenix, who brings daily inspiration to her children and a multitude of grandchildren and great grandchildren. At 88 years young, Dorothy continues to radiate a legacy of courage, strength, and dignity beyond the passing of her husband of 55 years, the loss of three of her eight children, and triumph over a stroke. Emanating from this legacy, Nancy celebrates Angel Flight ~ a Journey of Choice by sharing her stepping-stones of life choices in a spectrum of pendulum swings, from a childhood of alcoholic reality interspersed into an idealism of sacred choices, with rare poetic sprinklings of authentic wisdom.

Nancy Buhl
P.O. Box 173
Montrose, CA 91021-0173
buhl_nancy@yahoo.com

My Story

We are each on a journey of choice, consciously or unconsciously following lifelong conditioned beliefs, patterns, and behaviors of our parents, siblings, peers, coaches, and teachers. By the time we reach adulthood, these conditioned emotions of action and reaction are played out in marriage with our spouse and children and in the work environment, through our bosses and coworkers. As grownups we frequently play out childhood fantasies, wishes, expectations, and unmet needs.

How do we identify these unmet needs? How do we consciously begin new choices of holding on to what helps support our well-being and letting go of what no longer serves us? These universal truths occur regardless of culture, education, gender, age, or financial status.

When we begin to discover the divine tapestry of the multi-colored threads intertwining our individual and collective self, we can explore the universal rhythm of Mother Nature and the beat of our own dance. Tuning within to our unique design provides us insight into our soul's journey. The more we understand ourselves, the better we are able to see and serve our divine connections to others, whether manifest through challenges or celebrations.

Every moment provides an opportunity to embrace our essence with an understanding of growth and love. In sharing, we become blessings to help others empower themselves. As we open our hearts to these blessings, we honor an ageless heritage of ever-evolving spiritual truth. The trials and tribulations of our life give us insight into our stepping-stones of choice.

My journey is shared to celebrate our universal dance of vibrant colors, sounds, textures, and feelings in a blend of individual choices, forever connected and disconnected at the umbilical cord of our human existence. Please accept my personal invitation to join with me in celebrating Angel Flight ~ a Journey of Choice.

Nancy Buhl

Angel Flight ~ A Journey of Choice

Life Experience 101

Life Begins Before Birth. What unconscious lessons are ingrained in our soul before we even begin to enter this earthly realm of consciousness? What genetic blueprint of DNA defines the rules of the road cast in a legacy of cultural, environmental, and generational family patterns and conditions setting in motion our stepping-stones of choice? How do we begin to define our unique path in the midst of such overwhelming external absolutes?

My entry into this world was delayed because the doctor went on vacation; thus setting in motion a lifelong belief that everyone else was more important and that other people always came first. My arrival was founded upon generational patterns of alcoholism, unspoken love, steadfast and persevering work ethics, and a propensity for being strong-willed, referred to by some as stubbornness — a not unlikely happenstance from a family of redheads.

I have no recollection of childhood handholding or hugs, although later years provided remembrance of my dad rubbing Sloan's Liniment upon my aching legs due to the growing pains of my tomboy youth and a passion for sports. Another example of such a legacy occurred in 1984, when I created a volunteer position in the nursery department of a hospital to prayerfully welcome newborn children into this world. Whether cradling, singing, or embracing with a soothing touch, I celebrated these precious gifts, some of whom were addicted to their parents' transgressions or left to fend for themselves by adults who tossed aside their parental role.

Keys to Learning

- We can learn from generational behaviors, core beliefs, patterns, and feelings.
- Knowledge of the known is frequently the bridge to the unknown.
- Our experiences are often based on our perception.
- Another person will share the same experience with a different perception.

- Are you ready to come out from your past to play in your present?

Life Experience 201

The Role(s) We Play. The order of our existence plays a key role in defining how we play the game of life. What is the sequence of your birth, first-born, middle, or only child? Sibling rivalry establishes the ground rules of relationships played throughout life. Talk about peer pressure. Have you ever thought about how your childhood role translates into an adult role of parenting or remaining single? How do these roles manifest into the working world as owner or manager, entrepreneur, coach or mentor, team player or isolationist, at the top or the bottom of the corporate totem pole? Are the rules of the road pre-established or achieved by the norms of consensus and collaboration or originality and imaginative visions and decision-making? How do you define, respond, or react to these various roles?

I was born the seventh of eight children, the third of four girls. Early in life I had assumed a belief that everyone else was important and my job was to make sure others were happy and content — a common role in an alcoholic environment. Having frequently been told that I asked too many questions, knew too much, and was too sensitive; I learned to serve as a martyr of strength, courage, and responsibility, finding safety in an invisible world of silence. Listening and nurturing heightened my sensitivity and deep-held need to keep the peace.

My passion for kids is summed up in my favorite role in life, affectionately known as Auntie Auntie to 18 nephews and nieces and their incredible offspring. This special path unfolded for me at age 11. The challenge of geography impacts my connections but never disconnects my love for family. I am also blessed to spend time with children of friends and volunteering through the Youth Leadership Programs of Toastmasters International.

The concept of marriage did not occur to this self-actualized, independent-minded redhead. In 1986, however, Robert Buhl broke the mold of my predetermined perceptions. Suffice it to say, it would take an entire book to describe this tenderhearted teddy bear, from the inception of our 16-year relationship. It would also require that he receive equal opportunity to express his unique perspective of why he waited patiently for several years before I finally said, "I do!" Nine years after our special date on July 12, 1992, he still reacts with astonishment when recalling, "She said that I wasn't yet potty trained."

Keys to Learning

- Parents rule.

- Kids break rules.

- Siblings are great teachers (as cohorts, challengers, or care-givers).

- Past conscious and unconscious thoughts and behaviors rule our belief.

- For better or worse, we cannot run away from the past.

- We cannot change our childhood (we can change our perception of our childhood).

- Freedom and unconditional life can come from accepting that our parents did the very best they knew how to do based on their knowledge and experience at the time (we can also accept that of ourselves).

- A moment from now we might make different choices.

Life Experience 301

Agony of Death (Gift of Life). Regardless of background, we each experience the devastation and pain of loss. If we re-open our heart to the gift of life, the loss will not be in vain. Losing a loved one is an agony without description, preparation, or comprehension.

Traumatized by the death of my 19-year-old older brother Dan, my heart shattered into a million pieces of disbelief, powerlessness, anger, resentment, and guilt. My life force began to diminish at this devastating loss. At the same time, however, a tinge of gratitude surfaced that he had not gone off to the Vietnam War and had not suffered a prolonged illness or accident.

We all lived in a fog of unanswered questions. Why would God take such a loving, decent, and exceptional boy? How could Mom and Dad be expected to live beyond the loss of their son, an unnatural sequence of events? How could we find a reason, desire, and strength to celebrate life without our beloved brother? How could his friends from college continue their young lives, having witnessed firsthand his presence departing from earth, while they were talking with him?

Sitting on his bed at the dorm, he felt some chest pains and lay back on the bed and died. A cause for his death could not be determined by the medical examiner, adding to our pain, uncertainty, and fear. Have you ever experienced such a devastating loss? How did you deal with the betrayal and guilt?

A shining tribute was brought to life to help ease a portion of this shared pain as the Dean of Whitworth College in Spokane made an extraordinary exception to the rules by naming a hall after this incredible example of youth at its best. The Mullenix Hall stands as a unique legacy of this precious gift named Dan, an honor previously reserved for Presidents of the United States.

This earth-shattering event had a profound impact upon each family member, each finding our own way to fill this void in our heart. Our dad found the fortitude to return daily to his job as custodian at the college, at the very least an emotional turmoil of anguish and pride. At 18, I could not begin to comprehend why God was on a personal mission to punish me by taking my brother. The impact on my life is shared with you as a transition of stepping-stones, realizing that life is a process of ups and downs with a time to laugh and a time to cry.

At the age of 21, a car accident resulted in two broken feet and a broken knee, ending my dream of becoming a professional dancer. A tougher lesson came from releasing my self-protected high-wire defenses to accept the gift of friendship from Loretta and Gary Nicholson, which remains to this day, filling the void from losing my brother three years earlier.

The doctor also discovered that I was so anemic I should not be alive, ultimately helping me recognize that I had created a self-fulfilling prophecy of not feeling worthy of life. The cause of my thoughts, spoken words, and actions had created an effect of unworthiness. The lessons continued and through the teachings of Louise Hay, *You Can Heal Your Life,* I began to love myself, to envision different thoughts and choices, and to embrace my higher purpose. What lessons have you learned? How are you sharing your experiences?

In 1980, I ventured on a cruise referred to as the "Voyage of a Lifetime" to ancient sacred healing grounds. The dynamics of birth and death and the spiritual connection that bridges the perceived elements of heaven and earth through loving and eternal relationships enabled me to finally release my brother Dan with serenity and grace. I was also being prepared to unconditionally love and accept the passing of my father, in 1987, sitting with honor and gratitude at his bedside during his earthly transition. In 1993, our family released our dear sister Carol to her transcendence, losing her battle with lung cancer but whose courageous spirit continues to shine.

Another blessing occurred when I worked in the office of a group of critical care doctors. My desire to nurture responded to a call from the daughter of a patient, whom I had befriended on her many trips to visit her mom in the hospital. Wanting her mom's final moments to be secure in comfortable surroundings, they returned to their home. In this celebration of love, one night I took my harp to their home, prayerfully honoring God's presence with the gentle strumming of the whispering chords. I left their sanctuary around midnight, mother and daughter united in the sacred light of God's embrace. Her mom's passing soon followed.

Keys to Learning

*   Life is a precious gift.
*   We transcend loss by celebrating love.
*   Sharing understanding and pain can bring blessings to ourselves and to others.
*   With time, we can transform our pain into awareness and higher purpose.

Life Experience 401

You Are My Hero ~ Dear Macarena Mama. It took years of developing an understanding of unconditional love before I was able to recognize the sweetness of Mom's heart and the courage and strength she continuously showed in moving through and beyond her many trials and tribulations. A special remembrance was watching her recover from a stroke, in 1997, captured by my feelings of tenderness and pride.

You Are My Hero ~ Dear Macarena Mama

You are my inspiration
In oh so many ways
From sheer determination
In the passing of the days

In doing of the dishes
Until the job is done
With your hopes and wishes
Each moment you have won

It takes a little longer
To put upon your coat
I watch as you get stronger
And inspire that which I wrote

An exercising guru
With swings and just one more stretch
From spirit within so true
For which there is no match

Macarena hands are moving
From right to left of hand
The sashay is still behooving
As you turn and twist and stand

The glint of soul is shining
In the twinkling of your eyes
As you continue inspiring
From a truth so wise

My heart is touched so deep
As we share a smile of care
It's true at times I weep
For this flower so rare

Thank you, Mom, for being
Creator of my birth
I am truly seeing
The value of your worth

In God's Loving Light
Your Daughter Nan
December 1997

Nancy Buhl

Life Experience 501

Beyond the Fear (The Power of Choice). A time to laugh and a time to cry is how the story goes. A time to rejoice with the power of choice enables us to create our own unique journey, playing to our own strengths or weaknesses. Embracing our fears enables us to transcend limitations and barriers.

My fear of standing up in front of a group was based upon extremely shy childhood days in which my self-determined mission was to be invisible. With crystal clear recall, I return to a time in grade school when my capped tooth broke off and fell to the floor. I made an unsuccessful attempt to retrieve the tooth, which was eaten by my dog Blackie. The following day I still had to go to school and give an oral report, knowing that I would surely die of embarrassment from the broken tooth with blackened root.

Although I did survive the incident, the fear prevailed until 1992, when I sprang full-fledged into the world of Toastmasters International, a worldwide organization with a charter to help individuals improve their communication and leadership skills. Initiation by fire began when presenting my icebreaker speech, which opened with this: "I came from the land of the Spokane Indians, where I walked barefoot upon the land of my birth...." The timer incorrectly stopped me in the middle of the speech. I lived through the experience and began my path to self-confidence and self-esteem.

What type of childhood trauma or fear have you overcome? What ones are you still holding on to? I was in my 40s when I conquered this fear — an example that we are never too old...or too this...or too that...to change our life perception and rise above past restrictions.

Keys to Learning

- Fear is a powerful tool (we can choose for it to work for us or against us).
- Courage is a process of moving forward in spite of the fear.
- We hold the "Power of Choice" in our own hands.
- Choices create empowerment.
- Our choices make us happy or sad, grateful or resentful.

Life Experience 601

Living in Gratitude (Sharing the Journey). We don't always have choice over our experiences in life. We do, however, always have choice over how we choose to experience. *I Am a Child of God* was initially created to serve fellow travelers on a shared journey through, above, and beyond the disease called cancer. The value we place on anything in life helps determine our ability to experience and triumph over the outcome. I did not see myself as a victim or even a survivor of cancer, instead choosing to believe in a higher power to guide me in defining and claiming how to perceive my experiences and lessons.

My healing served as a stepping-stone to finally capture the gratitude I felt for my family. *God Created Aunties* became the title of a spiritual gratitude booklet that I created and shared with my family during our Thanksgiving dinner last year. At the head of the table sat our dear mom who received my tribute with customary humble heart, unaware of the gifts of her legacy. In person or in spirit, my dad, brothers and sisters, and nephews and nieces were each acknowledged for their incredible presence in my life. As usual, my dear husband contributed with the creation and sharing of my gratitude.

As the rising of the phoenix through the ashes, our tribulations would not be as meaningful without the trials. How do your values, experiences, and learning fulfill and transform your journey? A year after the surgery and radiation treatments, I've just been informed that the cancer has returned. In determining my next steps, I continue to claim my divine heritage. With the awareness that life is not guaranteed, I remain secure in the sanctuary of living each moment as a present from God.

Nancy Buhl

I Am a Child of God

I have also sat in this chair
Not so very long ago
With a feeling of despair
And just a touch of woe

I looked within my heart
Trying to understand
How I could fulfill my part
By placing my life in God's hand

United in prayer and light
For receivers and givers of care
Taking each step with God's might
Knowing my truth is to share

In truth, I see myself whole
Blessed by God's ultimate wealth
Fulfilling my sacred role
By claiming radiant health

In sharing with you my rhyme
Together, we'll take a stand
Claiming our health divine
Placing our life in God's hand

In Loving Prayer, Nancy
May 2000

Life Experience 701

Divine Tapestry of Love. Claiming a divine connection between myself and a multitude of caregivers, I created a poem entitled *In the Hands of Doctors* and another *God is Radiating Me with Love,* which I affirmed during daily radiation treatments. These external forces included an awesome array of doctors, nurses, technicians and hospital staff from the Kaiser Permanente Los Angeles Medical Center. Services expanded to include an incredible chiropractor, an intuitive acupuncturist, an enlightened massage therapist, spiritual counseling and a phenomenal love circle of family and friends. A belief in the Unity principles of self-awareness and responsibility, positive affirmations and the power of prayer served as my inner sanctuary.

We do not walk this journey alone. Role models of distinction who have enriched my path are: Oprah Winfrey, Chris Reeves, Nelson Mandela, Tony Robbins, Lance Armstrong, Maureen Greenberg, a dear friend who transitioned through her battle with breast cancer four years ago, and my dear sister Carol whose testament of courage and strength empowered my journey. From this heritage comes a reminder that each day is made sweeter as we create our own visionary blueprints. Through our collaborative spirit, we enrich the tapestry of our interwoven unique gifts and special talents.

As a council member of this incredible tribe of wise women who have collaborated on this book, it is my desire that you choose to receive this radiant torch and share it with your loved ones and those in need. If my journey strikes a harmonious chord with your radiant truth, embrace the circle of light. Until we meet again, I continue to celebrate each moment as a stepping-stone of Angel Flight ~ a Journey of Choice!

Journey Inward — Inspiration, Exploration, and Reservation

Britt Bensen, MPH, NIA

Britt Bensen is the President of Mwemba Mind/Body Health, a wellness and health care consulting firm in Portland, Oregon. Britt received her bachelor's degree in exercise physiology from Arizona State University and her master's degree in public health, health education, from the University of Arizona. She has a diverse background in Employee Wellness, Corporate Fitness, Breast Cancer clinical research and intervention, hospital-based health education, and campus health promotion. She is the author of *My Authentic Self: A Journey Through Journal,* a book devoted to self-care and the excavation of your authentic self.

Britt is Adjunct Faculty at Portland Community College, a clinical health care consultant and professional speaker in the area of mind/body health, and she conducts workshops and private healing sessions with individuals dealing with chronic illness, cancer, irritable bowel syndrome, and depression. Britt is an accomplished Nia Technique Facilitator, a Phoenix Rising Yoga Therapy Practitioner, a Somatic Facilitator, and holds American Council on Exercise certifications in Personal Training and Group Exercise Instruction.

Britt Bensen, MPH, NIA
Mwemba Mind Body Health
(503) 780-4034
britt@mwemba.com
www.Mwemba.com
To order *My Authentic Self: A Journey Through Journal,*
please visit www.Mwemba.com. or call (503) 780-4034 to order.

My Story

I grew up in Minnesota. I was raised in a small town.
My family is quirky.
I was sexually abused.
I was born and raised Catholic. I have practiced Buddhism.
I believe in human potential. My parents divorced.
My father had an affair. I forgive him.
Completely.
I have a brother I have never met.
He probably doesn't know I exist.
I used to confuse sex with love.
I have spent a night in jail. I remember it vividly.
I love ice cream. The real stuff.
My brothers make me laugh.
My mother inspires me.
My sisters make me proud.
We all embarrass one another sometimes.
I have fallen... a lot. I have gotten up more.
I live to dance. I love feeling sexy.
I am a healer.
Learning makes me feel alive. I am compassionate.
I was Bulimic for 12 years. I am over it.
I dig Madonna and Kenny Loggins.
Oprah "gets it."
Yoga calms my mind.
I sometimes still fall. I sometimes don't want to get up.
I went to college. I have a teddy bear named B.J.
I have harmed my body. I have healed my body.
I have a dog.
Most days, I like my body.
I sometimes feel unworthy.
I keep trying. I believe. I love. I trust. I feel.
I am an extraordinary, ordinary woman.
I am just like you.

Less than 10 years ago, I would have never dreamed that the woman I am now could manifest herself in this body. I cried a lot, was afraid of my own power, and seriously considered marrying a man who had been known to fight as passionately as he loved. I can remember a time I stood looking at myself in the mirror after another night of empty sex. I leaned in real close and said, "Way to go, Britt. You are exactly what you swore you would never be. You are worthless."

I was serious. I couldn't stand to look at myself with even a sliver of compassion. I didn't know who I was and I certainly didn't carry myself as if it mattered. Despite my mistakes, my lies, and my poor decisions, there was a voice inside of me that whispered, "There is more for you, Britt. What you have done is not who you are."

I held self-doubt, criticism, and hatred in one hand and a fragment of hope in the other. Beautifully, at the time I was feeling the most pain in my life, the most profound healer was introduced to me. The healer was Nia (pronounced NEE-uh). Nia, or Neuromuscular Integrative Action, is a healing arts program that blends dance, martial arts, and the body's wisdom to inspire us to heal our lives.

Choosing to make necessary changes in my life was supported largely by the gift of healing I received through my experience with Nia. Exactly how I came to know there was more for me in life I cannot say. However, I can say I heard my Spirit guiding me. I listened to the best teacher I know, my body. And I chose hope. The whisper inside me spoke of relief and sanctity. And I listened. I took tiny steps toward healing. I trusted the smallest voice inside of me. I trusted my Spirit to guide me.

Journey Inward — Inspiration, Exploration, and Reservation

Inspiration

```
        /\
       /  \
      /    \
     /      \
    /        \
   /_____\
```

Exploration   Reservation

Inspiration

What is inspiration? Inspiration is many things. It is breath. It is spirit. It is the gentle force at our back that moves us into situations that serve us and make us feel alive. When we look back at our lives, our most joyful, memorable experiences are likely to be those times when we were inspired by something or someone to become more than we thought we could be. In my case, the voice was largely internal. It was Spirit inside of me that invited me to believe I could align my beliefs with my actions. For many of us, inspiration only comes from the outside. This leaves us with a sense of vulnerability and inability to move forward without external support and prodding. When we are inspired from the inside, we experience an "a-ha" moment, in which we link who we are organically, soulfully to the direction we have chosen and we begin to move.

My inspiration guided me to form a women's group to go through Julia Cameron's *The Artist's Way.* I started doing yoga. I found a good therapist. I cleaned up my diet and sought counsel from a naturopath to avoid antidepressants and to get off the medications I was taking for migraines and ulcers. I slowly trudged out of what felt, then, like hopeless disenchantment and fear. I was inspired to move from where I was to a place that I knew would be better for me, and ultimately better for all of the people in my life. I ask you, what inspires you? From where does your inspiration come? Are you inspired from the inside out? Or the outside in? Who do you know who is self-inspired? What might you learn from that person?

Exploration

Exploration occurs when we begin to feel the weight of drudgery lift. We begin to be curious, playful, and intrigued by our thoughts, feelings, and emotions. We have evolved to a place where we embody the inspiration as a part of us and realize our personal power to ignite our own "a-ha" moments. Once we are inspired, movement begins. Movement, then, plants the seeds of value and we begin to creatively explore the strategies for healing we have selected and the experiences of those strategies.

For me, the benefits of working with a naturopath increased my energy dramatically and turned the ulcers in my stomach to butterflies. I began to welcome the mornings again. I would wake up with the birds and sit with my tea and journal before going to work. Slowly, I moved from hating who I had become to forgiving myself for where I had been and trusting that each day was a new beginning and an opportunity for me to find my authentic self. I recognized my exploration as a means to move closer to health and healing.

There was an intrinsic cycle to inspiration and exploration with which I had to deal. At times, when I would lose awareness of my role in self-inspiration, the momentum behind my exploration would wane and I would, again, feel sad and stuck. As I began to realize this pattern, I was able to use my awareness to intervene and re-stimulate inspiration through Nia and its supporting principles. Physically dancing my body inspired me to explore my dance of life.

Another important part of maintaining exploration was learning not to take myself too seriously. My mind has a tendency to yammer on and on about what is going on inside of me and how I got there instead of simply shutting up and moving forward. By consciously observing my thoughts, feelings, and actions, I slowly began to recognize the mental games in which I engaged. During the times when I felt stuck, I recognized that my body didn't know the difference between real and perceived fear, and I perceived a lot of fear. The judgmental voices in my head began to speak, "What if no one ever loves me?" "What if I can't hold down a job?" "What if I become an alcoholic like my father?"

I learned to dance through these moments. Again, inspiring myself through the healing power of the body and music. The in-breath was like a magnet. I would take a big inhalation and imagine a very strong magnet reaching deep within my body and attaching itself to the chatter. On the exhale, the magnetic breath would draw the craziness out of me and leave me with more space inside. I could feel myself letting go of the questions and trusting the purity of the breath. I would turn on music that supported my breath and healing movements for my exhausted body. Ultimately, my mind would settle and I would connect to the present moment and joy would replace the heaviness of my heart.

Through Nia, I have learned that beneath every emotion is joy. The body is inspired by itself when it moves and seeks to play, be well, and explore this life. I ask you, then, do you actively explore? How do you explore? Do you feed new situations with creativity? Playfulness? Curiosity? What attitudes and beliefs do you put in place so you are not let down when the exploration isn't what you expected? How do you detach yourself from the outcomes? How do you go about exploring your life?

Reservation

To reserve a space for myself, for my heart and soul, as I explore this life keeps me grounded, balanced, and connected to who I am and why I am here. Just as one might call the airline to reserve a seat for a flight, in this sense reservation is reserving a seat for ourselves in this life — not giving too much away. Finding a way to maintain an energy reserve in our bodies, minds, emotions, and spirits is integral to giving ourselves to the world. When we have an adequate reserve of energy, the contours of "Self" remains rich with nutrients and vitality. It is then we are most able to share our gifts with the world and find wholeness, laughter, and creativity in our lives.

In our culture, women have been instilled with the "helper gene." Although much progress has been made, we are still taught to give of ourselves to a fault. In my work, I see hundreds of women who are disconnected, unhappy, and exhausted. They have actively been inspired (generally by others' needs and expectations). They have been bold explorers of time efficiency and the lives of their families. They know how to get Suzie to ballet and John to soccer and make cookies for Mary's birthday party all at the same time *and* make sure everyone has clean underwear to wear tomorrow. But, what is missing is our ability to "reserve a seat" for our Selves on this trip called life.

Culturally, we have turned our focus on our Selves from function to mechanism. We expect consistent efficiency in our physical bodies and allow no room for ebb and flow. We are slowly losing our connection to the value of community and the human body as integral elements of nature. The mind is gaining increasing value, and the body is taking a back seat. Our physical activity levels have decreased drastically in the last century. We spend hours at a time sitting in front of computers, driving our cars, and watching television. Where socialization used to regularly include picnics, dancing, and barn raisings, we now meet friends for dinner at a local restaurant or for a movie.

We live in a capitalistic, patriarchal culture. America values the qualities innate to summer: happiness, productivity, and energy. We must be conscious to remember that still, quiet, and dark are not "bad" qualities, but rather as natural, and necessary, as their counterparts. In this culture, we have even gone so far as to disease the cycle of life by dishonoring the menstrual cycle and the submissiveness that often accompanies it. We treat menstruation as a dysfunction, masking our natural path of turning inward with drugs to force us out of our quietness.

Here is a story about the truest nature of reservation:

Two years ago, my husband and I made a winter trek up to Crater Lake, a national park in the mountains of Southern Oregon. We decided to live on the edge a bit and take the snowshoe tour, as the sun was shining. About 20 minutes into our tour, the ranger stopped and turned to the group.

"Do you see all of those sprigs of pine?" He waved his arm in the direction of a large clearing.

I squinted to see that every 20 feet or so there was a two-foot sprig of pine sitting on the snow. Someone said, "I bet squirrels or something drag them out in the sun to eat the pine nuts out of the cones."

"Nope," the ranger shook his head and smiled a bit. "Any other ideas?"

A woman in the back said, "Do the 75 mile per hour winds you were talking about break off the boughs and blow them out into the field?"

Again, the ranger shakes his head. He says, "Do you know what the average snow fall is per year up in these parts?"

A voice said, "Over 30 feet?"

The ranger nodded and leaned in to tell us the secret of the pine sprigs. His face animated, he said in a loud whisper, "Those sprigs you see are actually not sprigs at all. They are the tops of 20 and 30 feet tall living trees that are buried underneath the snow. That which you have called a field is actually a forest of young pine trees."

My eyes widened and something in me clicked. I realized that what I had experienced in my life a few years earlier was my very own cold, dark winter. I reminded myself of how the trees underfoot were just like me. They could do nothing but surrender to the cold. They didn't sit beneath the snow complaining of the winter's bitterness. They allowed it to be what it was. They embraced the season and used the time to rebirth and prepare for their exhibition of fruit and strength when the summer came. They did not question whether or not summer would arrive. All of their experiences proved to them that summer would, indeed, arrive — in its own time.

I, like the tree, had made it through my season of darkness by trusting nature. My intuition and past experiences reminded me to wait and listen for the whisper of summer deep within me.

For me, the Nia Technique has supported not only my ability to manifest self-inspiration and ruthless exploration, but it has also provided me with simple, tangible ways to practice recycling my energy and to stay grounded and in harmony with my environment. As a healer and a teacher, the greatest challenge I have found on my journey into healing in the inspiration — exploration — reservation triad is the reservation piece. I, like many women, struggle with giving too much of myself. As I have learned through Nia, the key to maximizing what I give and ultimately receive from the world is in staying consciously connected to the messages of my body. I am learning to listen closely for signs of imbalance and confusion in the body and heed these messages by re-evaluating my inspiration — exploration — reservation triad.

It might be said that inspiration is what moves us forward, exploration is what supports our being in the "now" and experiencing it fully, and reservation is what keeps us grounded, balanced and connected to the greatest good.

I ask you, then, do you hold a space for yourself on this journey we call life? How do you know when you have stepped over the line of giving too much of yourself? What do you feel in your body? Mind? Emotions? Spirit?

In this land of "more is better," we have come to realize that learning more and having more will inevitably bring us "more." What we have failed to recognize is that the path to healing is often not about the battle for more, but rather about clearing out of our Selves what no longer serves us. Healing is about creating space in the body, mind, emotions, and spirit so there is room and clear skies for peace of mind to enter.

For me, the Nia Technique has been the catalyst for my journey inward. It is the impetus for my work as a teacher and a healer in this world. It is rich with culture, deep wisdom, compassion, and playfulness. It has provided me the space to be internally inspired in my life, to explore my life's journey with curiosity, laughter, and integrity, and it has shown me the nonjudgmental value of reserving a space for my Self, for my healing, and for my Spirit so I may be contributing to the greatest good of my community. It has taught me, firsthand, that life is a dance. I choose the music, the steps, and the partner.

We are all women of strength and wisdom. We all have what it takes, deep within us, to be self-inspired, ruthless in self-exploration, and skillfully reserved. We all have what is necessary to excavate our most authentic selves.

To learn more about the Nia Technique, developed by Carlos Rosas and Debbie Rosas, please visit www.nia-nia.com. or call (800) 762-5762 or visit Mwemba.com.

My Authentic Self

My Authentic Self is a woman who believes in herself.
She is moved to action by joy and chooses to live each day with
eyes wide open and the curiosity of a child.
She clearly understands the value of self-care
and embraces opportunities to nurture her body, mind,
emotions, and spirit.
She knows that taking care of others is only possible
if she, first, has mastered taking care of herself.
My authentic self is a woman who acknowledges her light
and embraces her darkness.
She walks barefoot and believes in the power of her inner healer.
She is statuesque, regardless of her size.
She is a head turner and a breath catcher, even in her pajamas.
Her eyes reflect the universe.
Her laughter radiates compassion, self-respect, joy, and peace.
She recognizes herself as a source of unyielding healing
for the world. And she knows exactly where that healing
begins... She teaches this to the children.
Her hands represent the perseverance and strength required to
achieve fulfillment in stillness and quiet.
She is a human being.
She is a dancer of life.
She is wondrous, bountiful, beautiful, and complete.
She is her most authentic self —
and she has been within you all along.

CHOICES of the Financially Free

Loral Langemeier, MA, CPPC

Loral Langemeier, MA, Certified Personal Professional Coach, is the President of Choice Performance, Inc. Loral has been a strategic coach to thousands of people since 1989 in the area of peak performance. Her areas of focus for workshops and coaching include personal responsibility, business leadership, personal financial/investment strategies, and entrepreneurial growth.

Loral received her bachelor's degree in business administration and finance from Nebraska Wesleyan University; then her master's degree in human performance/exercise physiology from the University of Nebraska. Loral interned for Dr. Kenneth Cooper in the area of corporate wellness and human performance. She is an entrepreneur owning her own company from the age of 19; from 1990 through 1997 Loral worked as a consultant, then employee, for Chevron Corporation as an adviser for their employee health and productivity program. During that time Loral received additional training in organizational psychology and was certified as a Coach from The Coaches Training Institute.

An author and popular speaker throughout North America and Australia, Loral recently began a nationally syndicated radio show *CHOICES Live.* Loral is also the co-founder of Financial-Coaching.net; a company committed to expanding the financial well-being of humanity. Through Financial-Coaching.net, each client works on his or her beliefs/thinking about money and a personal plan for success. Loral is a leader in the coaching industry and contracts with many coaches to support "private label" coaching contracts with large organizations. Her personal, charismatic, bottom-line approach supports clients to get results in their business, finance, and personal life.

Loral Langemeier
Choice Performance
1135 Terminal Way, Suite 209
Reno, NV 89502
(888) 262-2402 or (415) 382-8466
(415) 382-8483 fax
info@choiceperformance.com
www.Choiceperformance.com
www.Financial-Coaching.net

My Story

On the fourth day after telling the biological father of my beloved son that I was pregnant, I learned he had just slept with his ex-girlfriend. It never occurred to me that I would be a single mom and that dark night in January 1999 would begin my journey of discovery. A discovery that led me to more courage than I ever thought was possible — a discovery that expanded my personal capacity further than I ever imagined.

I grew up in a large Midwestern family with very traditional values. I knew when I was 7 that I was special and here on this Earth to do something miraculous. The drive that God gave my spirit was deep and purposeful. Always active in learning and adventure, I knew the farm was not where I could stay. During college, I started my own health and fitness company. By the time I was 24, I had a successful corporate wellness firm. Accepting a contract to work on the offshore oilrigs, I soon went to work for a large corporation.

Freedom, spirituality, intellect, and adventure — those are the values I sought to honor. After working to get people healthy and sending them to a sick culture, I decided to go work on the culture. So after 5 years, I left the corporate world to launch Choice Performance, a financial and business consulting/coaching company. Living in San Francisco near the water where my soul is fed, I knew I had found home.

Because I was interested in wealth creation and financial freedom, my mentors Bob Proctor and Robert Kiyosaki imprinted on my being the "knowing" that it was all possible. A series of mentoring and "emotionally significant" workshops guided me to a powerful vision and confirmed purpose — being of service and coaching people to know what is possible for them in the area of finance and business — that's where it was juicy for me.

Now on my second career and living on purpose, I began doubling the company year after year. On target to be a millionaire by the time I was 35 — nothing was going to stop me. Until January 1999. How could I ever do this? How did I get off track? With all my drive and focus, how could I let a man of such low integrity and commitment get in my way? How could I be a single mom? The spiral of self-doubt and internal conflict was torture. The "forgive me" roller coaster ride lasted several months. In and out of a relationship with me and with his old girlfriend — lying, cheating, and manipulating for money.

On April 1, 1999, I took the most courageous stand of my life. Scared to death and alone, several friends packed my Durango and sent me to his parents with the last load of his crap. It was over, and I needed to take care of me, and of my child. After days of silence, I committed myself to being the most powerful single mom, AND I was going to stay on purpose with my career. I could create it the way I wanted. I could have it all. I was determined that this was all for a reason. I now had less than six months to create a solid foundation to financial freedom for my son and me.

Knowing that I wanted to take time off when I had my baby, I found a business partner, Will Mattox, to help grow the company and began an aggressive investment strategy. I was on my way back and determined to find the sources of support and strength to be an amazing mom. That summer I turned 35 just two weeks before my net worth peaked $1 million.

My sweet spirit, my son, was born on September 6, 1999. After a grueling 45.5 hours of labor with three dear women — here he was. My capacity to love was larger than anything I had ever experienced. I was also never more focused, committed, and dedicated to living out my purpose than the day I gave birth to my son. On that sacred day, God blessed me.

More than ever, I now had purpose, passion, and conviction to live a responsible, financially free life. My son's birth was not the beginning of this journey; it started when I was 7 years old. My son's birth taught me about capacity. We are granted all the choices necessary to be financially free — to not do so is a sin.

I want to share my CHOICES to financial freedom. I want to share the capacity that it takes to get there and stay there. Specifically, I want to share it with women, encouraging them to stand in power and choice. Take personal responsibility and make life what you deserve. Financial freedom *is* available to everyone. Make the choice now, today, and begin the journey.

CHOICES of the Financially Free

The Key to Your Financial CHOICES

Creating wealth and freedom is available to everyone. It is our God-given right to be wealthy. My hope is that people take their space and know they deserve it. Unfortunately, in our society many people learn from an early age that money is bad, dirty, only for evil people, and that we must work hard for it. I believe that money, sex, and God are the most important subjects for children to learn about and the three subjects never talked about in school.

Take a moment and reflect on this statement: "Money is…"

What did you think about? Most people say money is energy, spirit, fun, easy, creative, and so on. That's what most people "want" money to be. The truth is that money is hard, you have to work for it, it only comes monthly, rich people are bad, and you get the idea. The truth is seen in action. I can look at someone's calendar and checkbook and know what they are committed to.

Do This: Do a three-month review of your calendar and checkbook. Look for themes and patterns of spending time and money. Is this getting you the results you want?

Results are why most people come to financial and business coaching. Results are driven by actions, actions are driven by language, and language is driven by thought. The core of your results has been a direct impact on what you think. OR your thinking is the core impact on the results you have in your life. Don't like your results? Change your thinking!

How to get started —

• Your first CHOICE is to be clear about your purpose and to create a vision. PUT IT IN WRITING, with a time frame and specific accountabilities.

Most people do not have a clear direction or vision. Too many people are committed to current reality and thus spin around in circles because there is no "point A" and "point B." What I call the motivation gap occurs when the vision of what you want (point B) is clearly more compelling than current reality (point A). This gap is one of the most powerful ways to create motivation. AND you must get committed to "a better place."

Do This: What is the better place for you? What are you passionate about? Clearly articulate and write out your personal vision statement?

- The second CHOICE for getting started is to take stock of your current financial situation. Once this is in place, create a plan that leads to your vision. You cannot decide on where to go until you know where you are.

Let's look at the basic vocabulary for creating a financial statement. The personal financial statement identifies two areas:

- The first is your **assets and your liabilities,** which are reflected on a **balance sheet.** This is simply what **you own (assets)** and what **you owe on (liabilities).** Subtract your debt or liabilities from your assets and you get your **net worth.** It's rarely what you think. This is an ever-changing reflection of how well you are playing the money game. Know what you're worth! *Net worth = assets – liabilities*

- The second area on your balance sheet is **your income and expenses.** If this is done for a business it is called a **profit and loss** statement. This is a reflection of how much money you make and how much you spend.

If you subtract expenses from income, you get the **disposable income or your cash flow.** This is the money that you might spend on investment. Most people spend their extra monthly cash flow on personal, immediate gratification. **Cash flow = income – expenses.** It is crucial to know where your money comes from and how much. It is equally important to know where it goes. With the personal financial statement, you will have a clear picture of current reality.

Do This: Fill out your personal financial statement and notice what it is showing you. What are you worth? What is your monthly cash flow? What does this say about you and your life? What do you want to change?

- The third CHOICE for getting started is to look deeply at your beliefs. What we think about is what we create. What you expect is what you get more of. Our mind is composed of our conscious and subconscious mind. This is where all of our thoughts are impressed. When we are children, our subconscious mind is like an open funnel, and all that goes in will soon be the backdrop for our decision making. For example, if you grew up in a household with parents who consistently said, "We can't afford it, we live paycheck to paycheck, you have to work hard for your money," your subconscious will hold on to those thoughts.

So for instance, if you would win a million-dollar lottery, the conscious mind will perceive the million bucks coming in and get all excited — yeah, I won!! Immediately, the conscious mind MUST check in with the subconscious mind and will ask, "Have you seen anything like this before?" If your subconscious belief is "I live paycheck to paycheck," guess what? Your subconscious mind will create decisions and actions to ensure that you do. So, a million dollars may take a while to spend, yet what we know about millionaire lottery winners is that only 2% ever retain their winnings. You must make the CHOICE to know what you think — become aware of your self-talk.

Do This: Listen and record your self-talk for one week. At the end of each day, reflect on your thoughts and record them. Look for patterns and time spent on certain areas of thought.

Once you encounter negative thinking, CHOOSE TO CHANGE IT through this exercise:

Old Belief / Thought	New Positive, Present Affirmation
I live paycheck to paycheck.	Money is always available.
Money is hard to get.	Money flows freely and easily.

Make a list and then 50+ times per day for one month reaffirm your new positive, present affirmation of thought. Even if it feels strange, stay with it. Focus on what you want — your vision!

Creating your financial plan

Just like you have a plan for your health, your vacation schedule, your schooling, YOU MUST have a plan — and spend time on your money/finances — regularly. Having regular money habits is critical — and most overlooked.

Examine your desired financial state and ask yourself these questions: What are your specific objectives? What are your smart (specific, measurable, achievable, realistic, timely) goals? What is your timeframe? What is your net worth?

How much monthly passive income (cash flow) do you want in relation to your expenses? Most people have the hardest time with the "dream" — what you want it to look like, specifically, financially. This is where you will notice your "self-talk" and beliefs getting in the way. Your attention and expectation on money will give you insight into what is really important to you in relation to money.

The thing I learned in creating wealth is that your intention, expectation, and attention to money MUST get into focus. You cannot make a decision about what "to do" until you know what it is you want. So, go away to a beach, go take a long drive, find the time to get clarity on your desired financial state AND it must align to your vision. Be as specific as possible.

Notice that increasing income is NOT the only answer, yet most of us grew up in a society of get a good job, make more salary, get good grades, and so on. This is about financial intelligence — not scholastic aptitude. The tax advantages for starting a side business far outweigh the increase in salary. What do I do for a side business is your next question? I again ask you to dream — what do you want? Owning a business provides you with an asset, assuming you generate revenue.

List your expenses (monthly payments for your home mortgage, car, phone, food) and liabilities (what you owe on your home, your credit cards, car loan) and notice what you are "willing" to reduce or cut.

First, if you are severely in debt, watch if your thinking is about "getting debt free." Know that not all debt is bad — you have to be smart. For those who have debt, one formula is to list all your debt in order from the highest percentage of interest owed to the lowest and begin creating an aggressive plan to reduce the debt. Commit a specific amount of money every month to this process.

Then, when you have lowered the debt, continue that same "habit" and re-allocate that same amount of money to your asset column. Do not start spending again.

Second, if your plan includes a business (even a side business), you now have turned most of your expenses that you could never deduct as an employee to tax deductions. Your lunch out to discuss your business is now a pre-tax expense deduction, your computer and home office is now a tax-deductible expense, your vacation now includes a business meeting and is now tax deductible. Owning a business is one of the fastest ways to give yourself a raise.

Attention to your asset column

How have you invested in the assets now? Most people have none. As Robert Kiyosaki says in *Rich Dad, Poor Dad,* "Most people have a cash flow pattern of the poor or middle class." What this looks like for the poor is all the money coming in goes out to pay expenses, and the middle class typically increases liabilities (home mortgage, car payments, for example), which increases expenses, and still they have little monthly cash flow.

The asset column is where the wealth is. This **must** become your primary financial column of interest in creating your plan. Assets that create income create wealth and passive income (this is what I call mailbox money — you do not work for it).

Current Assets	Desired Assets
Company 401K	Roth IRA (commit to annual contributions)
Cash savings	Tax deed
	Small real estate deal (producing monthly cash flow) — within 3 years large real estate property

Continue your plan of dreaming and creating. The bigger your asset column — the greater your wealth. This is where most people do not have the "capacity" or tenacity to commit to delayed gratification. The principle of compounding money in your asset column is critical to know. The more you put away now into investments that either produce cash flow monthly, appreciate over time such as real estate, gas wells, tax deeds, and businesses, the faster your wealth grows — through up and down cycles of the market.

I know what you are thinking: "I don't know how to invest." Neither did I! Find people whom you want to aspire to — not those around you who have what you have. I know so many of my coaching clients get advice from family, friends, from people doing no better than they are. When I knew that I was going to become a millionaire, I knew I needed to start spending time with them. I wanted to know what they did — what were their habits? What did they read?

Specific strategies and rules

There is no magic pill or script — just like dieting — it is a committed lifestyle with increased capacity that will get you financially free and living at CHOICE. Strategies are basically your action steps — what will you do — by when — and accountability to your actions. Rules are the absolutes. Rules keep you true to your vision and strategy. If you think of it like a vacation, your destination is the vision, your car is the chosen strategy to get there, and road signs and maps are the rules that allow you to arrive safely.

Let me put this in personal perspective: My vision is to create financial and business literacy in the world. I have a clear picture of current and desired financial states. One of my strategies is to create a high cash flow business and then take a large portion of the revenues to invest in my asset column. Some of my rules include paying myself first, never touch any money in my asset column except to re-invest in another asset (in other words, I can't take money from my asset column to buy a boat or new car), and maintain monthly, passive cash flow greater than monthly expenses.

Your strategy could include starting a side business if you are currently an employee until the revenues are great enough for you to quit. Other options are these:

* Begin learning about real estate and how to do "no/low down deals."

* Research tax liens/deeds.

* Start your own portfolio in addition to the typical 401K (these are seen as investments and your employer controls it, so get some of your own control in your own portfolio).

- Join a network marketing company as a side business.
- Be the "deal maker" and find deals for people with money who do not have the time to look for deals.

Make a list of strategies to support your vision to wealth. Next to it list the rules necessary to achieve it:

Strategy	Rule
Get out of debt	Pay a specific, consistent amount every month. Only use credit cards when you pay 100% of balance each month. Research investment so when debt is gone — the habit shifts to paying yourself first (in your asset column).

With a clear vision and a plan that has strategies and rules clearly defined, you are starting down the path. Remember this is your plan. Allow yourself to be creative and flexible. In the beginning watch not to get "attached" to how it has to be — just get your intention clear that, no matter what, I deserve wealth and will have it. This is not ever at anyone's expense — this becomes a game of challenging yourself to see what your capacity is. Study those who are rich — there are very specific rules and principles. You will want these people on your team.

Your financial team: Who will help you get there?

List the five people you spend the most time with. Are these people on a similar financial path? If they are not, find five others who are doing and living the way you want. As you look for your team, consider people in the following areas: Financial Planner, Certified Public Accountant, Tax Strategist, Attorney, Real Estate Attorney, Incorporation Specialist, Millionaires — and multi-million-aires, and those who are successful in your area of focus.

Actually ASK these people for their support on YOUR PLAN. It is important for you to know if they will support you in your journey to financial freedom. Have them strategize with you. Show them the completed portions of your financial plan to explain where you are now and where you want to go.

Stay the course

Many people search for the content, the how-tos, the tips, the magic pill. Your CHOICE for financial freedom lies in your capacity to learn, grow and reach for what you deserve. Your context is what will enable you to absorb and be able to use that information. If you are not truly ready to accept your financial freedom, if you cannot really see yourself there, all the content in the world will not help you achieve your goals.

Challenge yourself to grow your context by examining its origin and surrounding yourself with success. Let's face it, you've had a lifetime of financial education. You are constantly being programmed about money in print, radio, television, and now the Internet. You have little control over what you have heard in the past, but what you hear from now on and how you regard that information is within your control.

Commitment creates opportunity for action! Write that commitment, then ANNOUNCE IT!

Start with: "The one thing I am committed to do today is:

_____
_____
_____

Do this every day and share this commitment with the five people who agreed to support you on your path to financial freedom once your plan was complete. Sharing locks in your commitment and puts it out into the world. There is no going back now. Sharing your plan and commitment also engages others in your energy and CHOICE for financial freedom.

Final thought: There is no lack of opportunity for wealth and abundance. Opportunity is unlimited. You therefore need not be competitive, it decreases you. Be creative instead! Creative increase starts with creative thought. You must focus your attention on yourself and not be concerned by what others are doing. Work on you, and let others be responsible for themselves. You must remain focused on the positives and not the negatives. This applies to thought, language, and actions. You must be grateful for all you have in order to receive more. People are naturally drawn to others who have created abundance without competition.

Turning Emotions into Strength and Passion into Success

Vicki D. Jones

Wife, mother, artist, entrepreneur, Vicki Dortch Jones turns life's lessons, passion, and faith into successful living and success in business. She learned it isn't easy to be a super wife, super mom, and super businesswoman, but it is possible — with controlled emotions, incredible passion, uncompromising commitment, and faith in God.

Born and raised in Longview, Texas, Vicki attended Kilgore College and North Texas State University before heading to Las Vegas where she received her Bachelor of Fine Arts from the University of Nevada, Las Vegas. She earned her Master of Arts from the University of Texas at Tyler and completed post-graduate work toward an MBA from Stephen F. Austin State University. After seven years in marketing and public relations, Vicki began her entrepreneurial journey, owning three art-related businesses concurrently. In 1988 she joined her sister, Seleta Dortch Lovell, as co-owner of Etex Medical Supplies after their mother's death. As sisters, best friends, and business partners, they became nationally known in home health care for their creativity and innovative business strategies.

Vicki learned through her mother's tragic battle with cancer that a woman's need for dignity and self-esteem is second only to life itself, at a time when she needs more than ever to feel good about herself. From this experience, she and her sister developed Women's Health Boutique — a beautiful shopping environment devoted to meeting the special health care needs of women. Building on this unique concept in health care, they expanded through franchising and founded Women's Health Boutique Franchise System, Inc., in 1993. Vicki wrote the Forward Message in *I Feel Like Me Again* by Nancy Arnold, now in its third printing, which tells the story of Women's Health Boutique and is dedicated to the memory of Vicki's mother, Billie Marie Dortch.

They sold the franchise system, but Vicki still owns and operates the original Women's Health Boutique in Longview and serves as a consultant for the franchise system. She is a board certified mastectomy fitter and orthotics fitter. She speaks nationally on women's health issues with a mission to touch women's lives and make a positive difference in attitudes and "altitudes." Her goal is to prove the incredible strength of a woman's emotions, the power of passion, and the inherent joy of being a woman, a wife, and a mother in business.

Vicki D. Jones
Women's Health Boutique
510 E. Loop 281
Longview, TX 75605-5000
(800) 525-2420
whblongview@aol.com
www.w-h-b.com

My Story

I was raised in a strong Christian family with parents who instilled love, morals, values, and respect in my brother, sister, and me. My father was a successful Chiropractor, but is an inventor, songwriter, and artist at heart. My mother was a successful entrepreneur at a time when few women were. But she also had a kind and compassionate heart, a winning personality, and truly lived the abundant Christian life.

As a child, a young entrepreneur, I always sold the most Camp Fire candy and the most tickets to everything. From cleaning my mother's rent houses, helping at my dad's office, delivering brochures for my mom's real estate company, to teaching swimming lessons, work was not something I had to do; it was a part of who I was.

More than a college degree

In college, I tried out for everything. When I didn't make the world famous Rangerettes, I believed it was because there was something bigger and better for me. Not making cheerleader was harder. After I won the Miss Hallsville pageant, I believed my destiny was to be the 1974 Miss Texas. I didn't win. I didn't even place. I entered pageant after pageant before winning the Miss Richardson crown in 1975. I rode in parades, made appearances, posed for pictures, and signed autographs for other young pageant hopefuls. In the 1975 Miss Texas pageant, I did win the non-finalist talent award for my Tchaikovsky concerto, but fell one short of the coveted Top Ten. With passionate fervor, I transferred to UNLV in Las Vegas intending to be the next Miss Nevada. I was a slender, 118-pound concert pianist. The preliminary pageant was 11 months later, and by then I was a rusty pianist weighing 140 pounds. I had tried every diet and weight loss fad in existence. As second runner-up, I decided that pageant was my last.

My pageant days were over but my entrepreneurial spirit soared. After graduation, I became "Rose Tiffany" at the Tropicana Hotel and Casino. Wearing pageant gowns, I sold long-stemmed roses and carnations in the Folies Bergere showroom, celebrity showroom, and gourmet dining room. A typical four-hour night would net $300.

I earned more than a college degree in Las Vegas. I came home with lifelong lessons that fueled my passion for life and ignited my compassion to help others.

A vision

I owned an art gallery and an advertising agency when my mother was diagnosed with terminal cancer. Hers was a rare, drug-induced cancer linked to Thoratrast, a radium dye she had been given 30 years earlier to detect blood flow. I'll never forget the shock when we heard those awful words: our mother has two to six months to live. I was seven month's pregnant with my second child.

Vicki D. Jones

My mother fought a hard and courageous battle for 17 months. She continued to build Etex Medical Supplies, her home medical equipment company, working right up to the day she went to the hospital the last time. She recruited my sister from her banking career to teach her the business. Seleta worked by Mother's side, month by month, then day by day watching the cancer destroy her body. To the rest of the world, family, friends, even me, Mother was strong and "felt great," but Seleta knew the truth. Mother felt she had to be strong for me with two babies. Seleta was strong for Mother. Mother lost her hair but never her dignity. Mother's goal was to die gracefully. And she did. May 25, 1987.

For the first year after Mother's death, Seleta ran Etex Medical and I helped with marketing and public relations part-time. When Mother's estate was settled, Seleta and I became partners in Etex Medical. I was expecting my third child. With two toddlers under age 3, a career change was challenging, but exciting. Combining my artistic abilities and marketing expertise with Seleta's knowledge of the business, we designed one of the first retail accessibility showrooms in America. Lacy was born two weeks before we opened.

I had fun. Instead of painting paintings, I painted lightning bolts of color on custom wheelchairs. Plain wooden crutches were painted psychedelic colors or splashed with a rainbow of primary colors. We displayed a hospital bed in a make-believe bedroom topped with one of Mother's quilts and bath safety equipment in a real bathtub. But most important, we treated our customers like family. We cared. *Homecare* magazine featured us on their August 1990 cover with a feature article appropriately titled "Etex Medical: Balancing Ministering with Marketing."

A wake-up call

December 19, 1990, was a day that changed my life. My sister was having surgery at 10 A.M., and I had promised to be at her side to pray with her before she went in. I stopped by the office first.

Christmas was a special time for us to thank our physician friends, nurses, and referral sources. We had pen and pencil sets engraved for each physician, and we had found the cutest half-pint mulling spices for the nurses. This was the day Tess was to deliver our gifts. Her blue Chevy Blazer was loaded to the hilt with hundreds of beautifully wrapped pen sets and mulling spices.

An urgent call came for a hospital bed, but Willie, our deliveryman, was already out on deliveries. My Suburban was often used as a backup delivery vehicle, so we loaded the bed and off Tess went. I would drive her Blazer to the hospital. As I was leaving, the phone rang. Instead of letting the answering service pick up the call, I answered it. The voice on the other end was frustrated to tears because the connection valve on her lymphedema pump was "stuck." I tried talking her through a solution, but she insisted I come and fix it. I looked at my watch. I had exactly 15 minutes to spare. Just barely enough time to scoot to her apartment, fix her pump, and scoot to the hospital.

I had her pumping her leg in no time flat. I jumped into Tess's Blazer with less than five minutes to spare. As I crossed the intersection at Judson Road and Delwood, my memory ends. From here it's a recollection of what others saw.

An 80-year-old woman turned left out of the right lane, plowing directly into the Blazer and sending it airborne. On the third flip the driver's door crashed 12 feet up the traffic light pole. I was not wearing a seat belt so the impact sent me crashing headfirst through the driver's window, over the traffic light, and onto the pavement. Over 50 feet. One eyewitness said I looked like a limp rag doll thrown through the air. Another wondered what caused the explosion of red smoke (mulling spices) and sharp flying objects. And yet another knew I had been killed instantly. Arnold Skinner stopped traffic until paramedics arrived. Back in his store, he called Gene Jordan at Longview Bank and Trust with the news, "Vicki Jones was just killed in a car wreck in front of my store." The news spread like wildfire.

Meanwhile my sister is refusing to go into surgery until I arrive and my father is pacing the floor of the hospital right by the emergency room door, expecting me to fly through any minute, late as usual. I flew through all right, bolted to a stretcher. My neck was broken.

I knew God spared my life for my three precious children, Crystal, Cassity, and Lacy, then ages 5, 4, and 2. I also knew God had something very special in store for me. I could have been a quadriplegic. Picture the headlines. "Former Miss America hopeful vies for a new crown, Ms. Wheelchair America." But God saw a different picture.

Miraculously, I only needed seven stitches in my head and a neck brace. Bruised from head to toe and horrendously sore, I was

Vicki D. Jones

allowed to leave the hospital 36 hours later, just in time to attend the funeral of our employee, Marty Thacker. Marty's death from breast cancer at age 39 coupled with my mother's death and my own near-death experience changed my business and my life.

A legacy

Marty had come into the women's boutique at Etex Medical Supplies just four months earlier inquiring about a job. She needed to work and a friend suggested she come see me. She longed for a place where she "fit in."

Following her mastectomy, Marty had developed lymphedema (chronic swelling secondary to lymph node removal after breast surgery) in her left arm. She always hoped no one noticed, but in her mind she could hear the whispers; she could feel the stares.

As I approached Marty, I knew what she needed most. I immediately put my arm around her and stroked her swollen arm. We hired Marty on the spot even though we didn't have a job opening. We never regretted that decision. Marty became our women's consultant. She had a keen awareness of women's special needs from first-hand experience.

Marty shared her horrible fitting experience at another local store. Tears streamed down her cheeks as she shared her brokenness as she brushed past beautiful lingerie she could no longer wear, only to be escorted to the owner's office for her fitting. I cried with her. I could feel her pain. I had watched my mother suffer the same emotions.

My sister and I vowed that afternoon to design a store just for women like Marty as a legacy to our own mother. An elegant, warm, and inviting store filled with products that would restore a woman's dignity and meet her special needs. Women's Health Boutique. Neither Marty nor my mother had any idea their deaths would inspire a business phenomenon that would touch the lives of women across America and eventually the world.

The world of franchising

Women's Health Boutique officially opened in February 1991. By the next year, women were driving for hours to shop in our beautiful boutique, designed for a woman's privacy and comfort. Our mission was "to meet the special health care needs of women and make a positive difference in the way women look and feel about themselves." Our story spread.

In 1993 we decided to expand and chose franchising because it allowed women to own their own business yet operate under our proven system. Seleta kept her focus on Etex Medical, and I devoted the majority of my time to developing the franchise system.

Our goals were overly optimistic and our venture capital campaign was a flop, so we started from scratch and bootstrapped our franchise system straight into the pages of health care history. I was driven by passion while my sister kept me tethered to the ground with reality checks.

I was at MedTrade in Atlanta, the world's largest home health care show, when I enthusiastically presented our franchise package to one of my mentors, Mal Mixon, President and CEO of Invacare Corp. He chose not to invest but he probably became the single most important influence in my personal success. I remember that day well. Mal told me that in order to reach our projections I would have to sacrifice my personal life and my family. I assured him I would never sacrifice my family for business. He replied that I was obviously not the entrepreneur I thought I was, to which I replied, "No, I'm not the wife and mother you thought I was." I was hurt. I didn't understand the truth he spoke that day. His wisdom was drawn from years of successful entrepreneurship. Mine was from naiveté.

In 1995, Seleta and I sold Etex Medical to a national HME company, which allowed me to concentrate my full energies on franchising Women's Health Boutique. We broke a cardinal rule for successful franchising. Our first 10 franchises should have been close to home. Our first was in Lathrup Village, Mich. In fact, our first eight franchises were scattered across six states from Michigan to Connecticut to Florida. That made training and support very costly. Since Lathrup Village was only 15 minutes from the Canadian border, I even got caught up in negotiating a master franchise license for Canada. With limited staff and resources, I would spend weeks at a time on the road. My life was a whirlwind.

One night, while saying bedtime prayers with my 7-year-old daughter, she asked me why work was more important than my family. She said I worked all the time and was never home and that "dads are supposed to make the money and moms are supposed to take care of the children." I remembered Mal Mixon's words and I cried.

I began the search for a partner in franchising. Bud Hadfield, founder of Kwik Kopy and ICED, and Steve Hammerstein, President of ICED, had been my franchise mentors for 14 months. In October 1996 we became partners and they put wings on my vision to make a positive difference in the lives of women across America. I remained President and CEO, but had to give up control over the system. For the next 18 months, my emotions peaked. I was frustrated, stressed, and out of town more than I wanted or needed to be. I felt responsible for the franchise system's struggles. In the spring of 1998, I was fired and ICED acquired full ownership of Women's Health Boutique Franchise System, Inc. I felt lost. Everything I worked and sacrificed for was gone. Again I remembered Mal Mixon's words. This time I prayed.

I revived my commitment to be a super wife and a super mom. At the same time, I devoted myself to growing Women's Health Boutique in Longview. My vision was renewed and my passion to help women soared. Once again, I balanced ministering with marketing. Women's lives were touched. I became a super businesswoman.

Today, with boutiques spanning coast to coast, it is my privilege to serve as a consultant to the franchise system and Bud Hadfield remains my dear friend. I owe him a debt of gratitude for giving me back my life.

Turning Emotions into Strength and Passion into Success

The lesson

As women, we play a powerful role in our society. We are nurturers and caregivers. We make 75% of health care decisions in America and control $2 of every $3 spent on health care.

Breast cancer gets our attention, but many diseases and immunological illnesses either disproportionately or exclusively affect women, such as cervical and ovarian cancer, osteoporosis, lupus, multiple sclerosis, eating disorders, and endometriosis. We have babies. We get varicose veins. We become incontinent and we live an average of eight years longer than men.

Consider these startling statistics.

- Cardiovascular disease is the #1 killer of American women. An estimated 500,000 women die each year of a heart attack or other heart disease.

- Lung cancer is the major cancer killer of women.

- Osteoporosis afflicts 50% of women over age 45 and 90% of women over age 75. It causes the death of 50,000 women annually, more than breast cancer.

We must take charge of our health care, of our lives. As women juggle career and family and care for aging parents, it is easy to get caught up in the super woman syndrome. As my mother would say, "And this too shall pass."

Let me share some tips for successful living that I've learned through experience, flavored with some "Billie Dortch truisms."

- **Control your emotions.** "Pigs get fed, hogs get slaughtered." When controlled, emotions are powerful. They are the prerequisite for passion.

- **Focus.** "Don't put off until tomorrow what you can do today." Creativity, , vision, and sacrifice allow you an entrepreneurial edge. But focus, order, and systems are required for success.

- **Exceed expectations.** "It's hard to be a woman in a man's world, but remember, you're a lady first." Be fanatical about things you believe in.

- **Always ask.** "They may say no, but they sure can't say yes unless you ask." A second opinion in health care is wise. A mentor in business is a valuable asset. Listen to both.

- **Go back to basics.** "Tithe 10%, save 10% and live off 80%." Have pride. Dream dreams. Believe.

- **Be accountable.** "What goes around comes around, in business and in life." Accountability makes us strive for excellence.

- **Never give up.** "When the going gets tough, the tough get going." Grasp a vision and never lose sight of it. Determination and persistence are the keys to success.

- **Learn from your mistakes.** "If at first you don't succeed, try, try again, and then try once more." Whatever point you are at in your journey through life, learn from your experiences, mistakes, and victories. And remember your life's experiences thus far are molding you for what you are to become.

Turn your emotions into strength and let your passion and faith lead you to success in life.